Further praise for *Bambi vs. Godzilla*

'Precise, scathing and perceptive' Lee Child, *The Times*

'Mamet skewers with precision and wit the rush for the buck that has become symptomatic of modern movie-making' *New Statesman*

'Astute, engaging and funny' *TLS*

'A collection of wise and incisive essays' *Sunday Times*

'Mamet's outrageous insider anecdotes make this an entertaining and provocative read for any movie lover with half a brain' *Metro*

'A subversive look at Hollywood's inner workings, tackling long-unanswered questions on every aspect of film-making . . . Behind the cosmetic touch-ups, movie-land is more cut-throat than you could possibly imagine' *Daily Express*

'It's as a stylist that Mamet is best known, and it's his style that distinguishes these essays' *Scotsman*

'Mamet the writer is at his best in this sparkling book: sharp, thoughtful, humane, and ironic' *Literary Review*

'Mamet is agreeably sharp-tongued and his far-reaching analysis probes the heart of ~~~~~~~~~~~~~~~~ His wit whets his derision to a keen edge

PLAYS

The Voysey Inheritance
  (adaptation)
Faustus
Boston Marriage
The Old Neighborhood
The Cryptogram
Oleanna
Speed-the-Plow
Bobby Gould in Hell
The Woods
The Shawl and Prairie du Chien
Reunion and Dark Pony and
  The Sanctity of Marriage
The Poet and the Rent
Lakeboat
Glengarry Glen Ross
The Frog Prince
The Water Engine and
  Mr. Happiness
Edmond
American Buffalo
A Life in the Theater
Sexual Perversity in Chicago
  and The Duck Variations

SCREENPLAYS

Oleanna
Edmond
Glengarry Glen Ross
We're No Angels
Things Change
  (with Shel Silverstein)

Hoffa
The Untouchables
The Postman Always Rings
  Twice
The Verdict
House of Games
Homicide
Wag the Dog
The Edge
The Spanish Prisoner
The Winslow Boy
State and Main
Heist
Spartan

NONFICTION

Jafsie and John Henry
True and False
The Cabin
On Directing Film
Some Freaks
Make-Believe Town
Writing in Restaurants
Three Uses of the Knife
South of the Northeast Kingdom
Five Cities of Refuge
  (with Rabbi Lawrence Kushner)
The Wicked Son

FICTION

The Village
The Old Religion
Wilson

DAVID MAMET

Bambi vs. **GODZILLA**

ON THE NATURE, PURPOSE, AND PRACTICE OF THE MOVIE BUSINESS

POCKET
BOOKS

LONDON • SYDNEY • NEW YORK • TORONTO

First published in Great Britain by Simon & Schuster UK Ltd, 2007
This edition first published by Pocket Books, 2008
An imprint of Simon & Schuster UK Ltd
A CBS COMPANY

Some pieces in this book were originally published in slightly
different form in the Guardian. Portions of this book are based on
the article "Bambi v. Godzilla," which originally
appeared in Harper's in June 2005.

1 3 5 7 9 10 8 6 4 2

Simon & Schuster UK Ltd
Africa House
64–78 Kingsway
London WC2B 6AH

www.simonsays.co.uk

Simon & Schuster Australia
Sydney

A CIP catalogue record for this book is
available from the British Library

ISBN: 978-1-41652-597-4

Printed by CPI Cox and Wyman, Reading, Berkshire RG1 8EX

THIS BOOK IS DEDICATED TO BARBARA TULLIVER

Douglas Fairbanks received me immediately and within a few minutes I was in his Turkish bath. This was the sort of club for the male members of high Hollywood society . . . it was a place where one lounged and steamed and heard the gossip. That day, besides ourselves there was Jack Pickford, Mary's brother, pale and slightly puffy but otherwise unmistakably a Pickford, a strange reputed Red-Indian being called Chief Longlance, and a number of the great moguls who shall be nameless because they were unbeautiful. In fact their sedentary and successful lives had made them old and fat as I am now.

—IVOR MONTAGU,
With Eisenstein in Hollywood

CONTENTS

Introduction   xi

x

CONTENTS

INTRODUCTION

All the rivers flow into the sea. Yet the sea is not full. Films, which began as carnival entertainments merchandising novelty, seem to have come full circle. The day of the dramatic script is ending. In its place we find a premise, upon which the various gags may be hung. These events, once but ornaments in an actual story, are now, fairly exclusively, the film's reason for being. In the thriller these events are stunts and explosions; in the horror film, dismemberments; in the crime and war films, shootouts and demolition. The film existing merely for its "high spots" has, for its provenance, the skin flick.

This deconstruction of the film as drama is the reverse slope, of which the ascendant was the genre picture. The genre film meant reassurance to the audience. They knew what they were going to get. They went into the theater, thus, to see Bette Davis, Joan Crawford, Dirty Harry, James Bond, John Wayne, Sylvester Stallone much as they might have gone to a pornographic film or, for that matter, to a stock car race.

Today, studios bet their all upon the big-tent franchise film, which is to say, upon appeal to a self-selected, preexisting audience. It is increasingly difficult to market the nonquantifiable film, as the franchise model continues its advance toward total control of the studio's budget and, thus, of the market. For all industries migrate toward monopoly, and decrease in competition inevitably results in decrease in quality.

Phenomena, when they can't get bigger, get smaller. There are wheels within wheels, and the big wheel runs on faith, and as we know, the smaller runs by the grace of God. The hucksters who invented the nickelodeon and the hucksters who administer its present incarnation are sisters beneath the skin; we, the artists and craftspersons, then as now, tear our flesh and rend our garments, bemoaning the tin ear and the monstrous cupidity of those same hucksters.

After the conflagration, in the final years of humankind, the artists will, once again, be found painting the ceilings of the caves, and the middlemen will, as always, be trying to talk the honest hunters out of their kill. And it may or may not then be remembered, or indeed believed, that there was once a time when the two groups were inextricably linked.

THE GOOD PEOPLE OF HOLLYWOOD

HARD WORK

Billy Wilder said it: you know you're done directing when your legs go. So I reflect at the end of a rather challenging shoot.

The shoot included about five weeks of nights, and I have only myself to blame, as I wrote the damn thing.

Directing a film, especially during night shooting, has to do, in the main, with the management of fatigue. The body doesn't want to get up, having had so little sleep; the body doesn't want to shut down and go to sleep at ten o'clock in the morning.

So one spends a portion of each day looking forward to the advent of one's little friends: caffeine, alcohol, the occasional sleeping pill.

The sleeping pill is occasional rather than regular, as one does not wish to leave the shoot addicted. So one recalls Nietzsche: "The thought of suicide is a great comforter. Many a man has spent a sleepless night with it."

One also gets through the day or night through a sense of responsibility to, and through a terror of failing, the workers around one.

For folks on a movie set work their butts off.

Does no one complain? No one on the crew.

The star actor may complain and often does. He is pampered, indulged, and encouraged (indeed paid) to cultivate his lack of impulse control. When the star throws a fit, the crew, ever well-mannered, reacts as does the good parent in the supermarket when the child of another, in the next aisle over, melts down.

The crew turns impassive, and the director, myself, views their extraordinary self-control, and thinks, "Thank you, Lord, for the lesson."

The director, the star players, the producer, and the writer are *above the line;* everyone else is *below.*

There is a two-tier system in the movies, just as there is in the military. Those above the line are deemed to contribute to the fundability or the potential income of the film by orders of magnitude greater than the "workers"—that is, the craftspersons—on the set, in the office, or in the labs.

On the set, the male director is traditionally addressed as "sir." This can be an expression of respect. It can also be a linguistic nicety—a film worker once explained to me he'd been taught early on that "sir" means "asshole." And, indeed, the opportunities for tolerated execrable behavior on the set abound.

I was speaking, some films back, with the prop master about bad behavior. He told me he'd been on a film with an ill-behaved star who, to lighten the mood or in a transport of jollity, took to dancing in combat boots on the roof of the prop master's brand-new Mercedes. "He did about ten thousand dollars' worth of damage," he said, "and this kind of hurt, as I'd given up my day off, unpaid, to go searching for a prop."

There exists in some stars not only a belligerence but also a litigious bent. I have seen a man take a tape measure to his trailer, as he suspected that it was *not quite* perfectly equal (as per his contract) in length to that of his fellow player.

Meanwhile, back at the ranch, the prop master is giving up his day off to ensure that the wallet or knife or briefcase or wristwatch is perfect on Monday.

This is not a picayune instance but, in my experience, the industry norm. While the star is late coming out of the trailer, while the producer is screaming obscenities on the cell phone at his assistant regarding, most likely, a botched lunch reservation, the folks on the set are doing their utmost to make a perfect movie.

I do not believe I overstate the case.

Nevil Shute wrote a rather odd book called *Round the Bend.*

Its hero is an Indonesian aircraft mechanic. He is so dedicated to both his job and the ideal of aircraft maintenance that a cult springs up around him. He is taken as an example as a teacher and then as the avatar of a new religion. In the practice of machine maintenance, he has found (and Shute closes with the notion that he may have *become*) God.

Some business people feel that they can craft a perfect (that is, financially successful) film *in general,* absent reverence, skill, or humility, and inspired and supported but by the love of gold.

But the worker is actually involved, as Leo the Lion says, in *ars gratia artis* and takes pride in working toward perfection through *the accomplishment of small and specific tasks perfectly.* Like Shute's hero.

Is the actor's hair the correct length? (The two scenes are viewed by the audience seconds apart but were shot months apart. If the hair does not match, the audience will be jolted out of the story.) Are the villain's eyes shadowed perfectly? Does the knife show just the right amount of wear?

I recall the homily of old, that thousands worked over years to build the cathedrals, and no one put his name on a single one of them.

We, of course, enjoy films because of the work of the identifiable, the actors, but *could* not enjoy them but for the work of the anonymous, the crew.

The crew is working in the service of an ideal. Faced, as they often are, with intransigence, malfeasance, bad manners, and just plain stupidity on the part of the above-the-line, they react with impassivity.

This might be taken for stolidity by the unobservant or self-involved. It is, in effect, pity.

I was taught early on that the dark secret of the movie business is this: *All* films make money. Their income, indeed, flows from on high, and the closer one is to the height of land, the more one gets. The farther from the source, the poorer. This is the meaning of the term of art "net profits," which may be loosely translated as "ha, ha."*

And just as there is gold in them thar hills (proximity to the source of the income stream), there is gold in the reduction of hard costs. This reduction includes legitimate business oversight, and may even extend, I have been told, to actual malversation of funds.

Also, we know of Pharaoh that he taxed the Israelites with harsh and unremitting labor, having them make bricks to build his palaces. He then decreed that they must gather their own straw. As did the Reagan administration when it killed the American labor movement.

The guilds and unions in the American film industry retain some strength and have the clout (at least in theory) to protect their workers against the depredations of management in that constant calculus of terror: Management: Submit or I will make all films in Hungary. Labor: Submit or we shall strike.

For any business folk in any business would be glad to take the workers' work for nothing—they, in fact, consider it their right. They would, in American films, as in hard industry, be

---

* Q. From whence does the money originally come? A. We recall the ancient Jewish wisdom, "If you look hard enough, *everything's treif.*"

right chuffed to see the workers race each other to the bottom, and then, having impoverished them, take the work out of the country. (As, in fact, the studios do now, shooting, I believe, the majority of American films elsewhere.)

The unions, in addition to protecting their membership against the money, must also protect them against their own love of the job. For in the practice of the movie crafts, we see the rampant American love of workmanship—and just as the true actor loves to act, the true carpenter or seamstress loves that perfect corner.

The American icon, for me, is *Rosie the Riveter*. Norman Rockwell's wartime masterpiece shows a young aircraft worker in her coveralls eating lunch. Her scuffed penny loafers rest on a copy of *Mein Kampf*.

Rosie the Riveter beat Hitler. Or, to be a little less high-flown—and in deference to the British, who were, as everyone knows, also involved in that late unpleasantness—there is a true and admirable American instinct of "getting it right."

As I was musing on the same, pondering the star, paid twenty million dollars and ruining the roof of a car, and the prop master, paid twenty thousand and giving up his one day off for the beauty of the thing, I believe I actually began to understand Marx's theory of surplus value: Q. Whom is the film "by"? Spend a day on the set and you learn. It is by everyone who worked on it.

PRODUCERS

My father was a negotiator. He opined that to conserve good feelings at the bargaining table, one should, if possible, express a negative concept in a positive form: "not meaningful" rather than "meaningless." I agree and will, therefore, now refer to contemporary movie executives as running around "like chickens without their heads cut on."

So much for humor. Now for the weather.

Life in Hollywood seems to have ground to a standstill. We have fewer and fewer films, and these are of diminishing worth and ever-inflated production costs. It is enough to drive one to the fainting couch.

There, whilst recruiting myself, I recur to my all-time favorite, Gérard de Nerval, who walked a lobster on a leash through the Tuileries. Oh, better than your pale shade Christo, I reflect, you have died too soon, a life dedicated to the exquisite remembered but in the admiration of those with much, much too little to do. Drift, then, my hand, from the scented kerchief on my forehead, to the low and accommodating bookcase but nearby. Roam, fingers, down those spines, so worn, so warm, the comfort of my grizzled age.

What have we here?

It is a novel by Captain Frederick Marryat: *The King's Own* (1831). See how the page, absent intention, falls open to a passage that may both mimic and direct my thoughts:

"Since the World Began, history is but the narrative of kingdoms and states progressing to maturity or decay. Man himself is but an epitome of the nations of men. In youth all energy, in the prime of life all enterprise and vigor; in senility, all weakness and second childhood. Then, England, learn thy fate from the unvarying page of time."

And there we have it, Spengler's two turgid volumes reduced to a mere paragraph.

Substitute "the movie business" for "England," and the thing is clear: that energy of youth, that cunning of age, must and will decay. Vigor itself will bring about death, for healthy life both breeds competition and attracts dependents—the necessity to still warring and to support legitimate claims distracts energy from the original healthy task of growth, and the walls come tumbling down.

The movie business, originally the *cosa nostra* of arcade hustlers, grew into fierce, healthily warring factions who now compete and now collude in a war fought not in the theaters but in the boardrooms.

I pass a poster for the current film and count eighteen names of producers.

On the poster?

Note that the poster is traditionally a way to attract the eye, and so the mind, to a novelty. The producers may in fact have contributed something to the film, but who in the world has *ever* gone to a film because of the identity of a producer? *No one*.

Then why list eighteen?

And here we have, to the physician, the unfortunate, inescapable, symptom—here is the sunken cheek, the dark hollow neath the eye, the foul breath and thready pulse, the herald of death: the film, perhaps, is being made no longer to attract the audience but to buttress or advance the position of the executive.

King Lear (read: Harry Cohn, B. P. Schulberg, Louis B. Mayer, Irving Thalberg) has gone to his reward, and his absence has been noted and acted upon by the canny. It is not that the fox has taken over the henhouse but, if I may, that the doorman has taken over the bordello.

In the golden days of the madam (Harry Cohn et al.), the lives of the girls may not have been better, but the lives of the customers were. Why? Because the owner-proprietor knew that her job was simply and finally *to please the customer.*

Moviemaking is an appallingly simple process. One needs a camera, film, and an idea (optional). The business of the movies, similarly, is simple hucksterism: find an attraction, present it as engagingly as possible, take the money, and guess again.

Just as the making of the film requires little more than someone to hold and someone to stand in front of the camera, so the business end requires nothing other than someone to make decisions. These decisions require intuition and/or courage, for the desires of the audience cannot be quantified; they may only, finally, be guessed at. The owner-proprietor, betting his own money, realizes that he is only rolling the dice. He stands to gain much, he stands to lose much, but he *has* to put his money on the street—that is, he has to place his bet. To that end, he strives to keep costs down, thus enhancing his chance at a greater time at the tables.

Current executives, however, have incentive to *inflate costs as much as possible,* thus necessarily minimizing the number of films produced (bets placed).

No one would think that way if he were gambling with his own money. But this new breed is not. They have tied their fortunes not to the success of a film, or of films, but of their superiors. They know that their superiors, the studio heads, will each, in time, be fired when the banks or the megaliths tire of their eventual failure. (Each must eventually fail, like the gambler who is shackled to the gaming table. *Eventually* the odds, in favor of the house, will clean him out. And for the studios the odds are, at the end of the day, in favor of the *audience*. The whims of the audience, that is, will and must break the studios, *if* the studios keep doubling their bets.)

The wise player of days gone by took his winnings and retired to a teenage wife and tennis in Malibu. Today's moguls, though, like the besotted gambler, keep doubling up. That is, they keep increasing their production costs. These increased costs propitiate not, primarily, the audience but the studio owners. "How can I take the rap for the failure of this film when I got the most expensive stars and sets and director possible?" is the exculpatory chant of the executive. "Let me try again."

The folly of this course is like that of the loser at roulette. He plays black, black loses, he doubles the bet and plays black again, black loses, he doubles his bet and plays black again. It loses. He reasons that soon black *must* come up—that the odds of red appearing five, six, seven times in a row are astronomical. Black *must* come up soon.

In his panic, however, he forgets two things:

1. His bankroll is not inexhaustible. Yes, the little ball must eventually land on black, but it might not do so until one spin after the player has gone broke.
2. The roulette wheel (like the audience) has no memory: the wheel is not aware that red has come up twelve times in a row. The odds of its appearance on the next spin are still 50-50.

The play rushes toward its dénouement. Films cost more, their increased costs attracting bevies of the sychophantic, for the larger the budget, the greater the possibility—indeed, the necessity—of waste. (The Pentagon could not, year after year, keep increasing its bloat if it did not, year after year, exhaust its stipend.) These executives scheme to hire, each and logically, his own retinue of supporters. And the gold-encrusted howdah must eventually drag down the mighty elephant.

VICTIMS AND VILLAINS

Are there *good* producers? Yes.

I met Otto Preminger in his office on Fifth Avenue. The setup was everything one might wish for in a meeting with a potentate-producer. The room was huge, and the desk might have been fashioned from the flight deck of a small carrier. He offered me a cigar. We chatted about this and that; he took me to lunch at "his" place on Fifty-fifth Street. At the end of the lunch he looked intently at me and asked if I had ever done any acting. I allowed that, yes, in my youth. . . . He nodded. "I'm looking for a young man to play an Israeli officer in my next film," he said. "Yes . . . might you consider it . . . ?" I was, of course, flattered beyond measure—that this great producer had seen into my inner soul, had seen my innate valor, strength, and capacity for both self-sacrifice and leadership. . . . "And there's something else I'd like you to consider," he said, and the something else was, of course, the kicker.

I have forgotten what service he was trying to extort out of me with his flattery, but I do remember he came damned close to doing it.

It was at this same lunch that he told me how he shot the vast crowd scene in *Exodus*. The scene is the proclamation, in Independence Square in Jerusalem, of the state of Israel.

Preminger required a packed square, some ten thousand extras. He could not pay for them.

"What did you do?" I asked.

"I charged them," he said. He papered the town with posters: BE IN A MOVIE, TEN SHEKELS. That's what I call a producer.

Preminger's dexterity in working with a limited budget puts me in mind of a situation we faced when I was directing my first film, *House of Games* (1984). Its producer was my friend and mentor, Mike Hausman.

We did the film for no money and, after a search for a suitably run-down inexpensive venue, chose Seattle. Seattle at that time was an other-than-affluent city and boasted a spectacularly seedy skid-row district, where we had hoped to shoot the film.

Here was the problem. Seattle was cheap to shoot in, but as it was virtually undiscovered as a location, all the equipment had to be schlepped up from L.A. The Teamsters Union had a rule that a film company would pay their members the going rates and benefits of that venue from which their drivers drove the equipment trucks. Their local rates in Seattle were just within the film's budget, but those of L.A. would have made filming financially impossible.

Mike scratched his head for a while, put the equipment trucks on railroad cars, and shipped them to Seattle.

We started filming, the Teamsters said, "Wait a second . . . ," and by the time the thing was adjudicated we had the film in the can. Mike and the Teamsters parted friends, and mutual respect, one pirate for another, was the order of the day.

Another great producer, Sarah Green, made several films with me in the Boston area. People bitched and moaned about the locale's intractable Teamsters, but we all got along just fine.

I made a film *about* the Teamsters (*Hoffa*, screenplay by me, directed by Danny DeVito), and the film, at the time of its release in 1992, got slammed by the press for, as near as I can interpret it, a pro-labor stance. I was accused, as writer, of being an "apologist" for the Teamsters.

Funnily enough, I didn't think the Teamsters needed an apologist, as they had a *union* (a much better idea).

The money people have been bitching about the Teamsters since the Lumière Brothers schlepped out the first camera, but as a member of various unions and guilds accustomed to handwringing, I admire the Teamsters' pluck.

Capital, if it cannot call Labor "Reds" *will* call it "Thugs." Actors' Equity, SAG, and, to a somewhat lesser extent, the Writers Guild, are addicted to going "Wee wee wee all the way home."

The Money suggests: "Give in: I can get *anybody* to act, you have no power," and the artistic guilds seem to perceive some truth in this suggestion, thus weakening their position.

They might reflect that anyone can drive a truck.

But back to Otto Preminger.

I was watching Preminger's *Exodus* the other night. There we have Paul Newman, who has my vote for the most beautiful man ever to grace the screen. He is fighting for the rights, for the lives, of Jewish refugees from Europe. Man. I love Paul Newman in this movie. He "just don't care." He doesn't care for the good opinions of the other players or, as per the script, of "the world." He endeavors to teach Eva Marie Saint, the love interest, a goodwilled American Christian woman, that nobody but the Jews cares about the Jews. This lesson is not only dramatically interesting but, in a rare coincidence, true. I sit there nodding.

Eva Marie Saint is terrific. She is, as above, goodwilled, sincere, and incredibly naïve. Quintessentially American, her answer seems to be, to everyone, "Is there not good and bad in all peoples?" Can't we just all "like each other"?

Paul's girlfriend, before the story began, got kidnapped from her kibbutz. She was, we are told, tortured, blinded, raped, her hands and feet cut off, and deposited back with her people, where she died. They name the kibbutz after her. Life goes on, and Paul has a one-night stand with Eva Marie. The next time he sees her, she reports that she regrets their fling; she is just a tourist and took a "wrong turn that night." Why? Because the young woman refugee she has grown fond of has elected to stay on the kibbutz rather than return to America as Eva's adopted daughter. Eva, in effect, "just doesn't understand these Jews." How, in effect, can they prefer each other to the company of an actual American?

The answer is, of course, that to Otto Preminger, to Leon Uris, who wrote the book, to Paul Newman, it is a fact of nature that the Americans "go home": that it is at this that we excel. Eva's foray into global politics is a prototypical example of what has come to be known as "adventure tourism." She will, pardon my French, get laid, "do good," become disenchanted, and go home (cf. Vietnam, Kuwait, and, watch-this-space, Iraq).

Exodus was a big hit. The theme music was played at every bar and bat mitzvah and Jewish wedding of my youth. They were playing our song. And lo, coincidentally, there we had this actual new country, scant time zones away, the first Jewish state in two thousand years, to go with the song and the film.

The music from *The Godfather* has also become an American racial staple.

The Godfather is ostensibly about a bunch of murderous thugs. Operationally, though, it is our American House of

Atreus. It is the story of an American family. It has gods, demi-gods, fates, furies, clowns, just like your family and mine. The family in question happen to be criminals. This is not only dramatically acceptable but also historically approved convention. The mafiosi are merely the Plantagenets of our day: removed, exalted, unbound by law.

Kay, played by Diane Keaton, is in love with Michael Corleone, heir to the mafia crown. He tells her he is going straight, and she responds that if he thinks she will believe him, he is naïve.

"We're just like presidents and senators," he tells her.

"Presidents and senators don't kill people," she says.

"*Now* who's being naïve?" he responds.

In both *The Godfather* and *Exodus,* the majority culture is represented by a legitimately nice, indeed, a lovely and good-willed, Protestant woman: "Why can't you" (Michael Corleone, Ari Ben Canaan) "just be like *me*?" the woman asks. The answer, in both instances, is that the hero is fighting for his life and for the life of his people, and the woman is not.

Now, *The Godfather* is, of course, the better film. Even its theme song is (marginally but nonetheless) better than that of *Exodus,* and to retire the trophy, the last time the Jews and the Italians clashed (Masada, 73 CE), the Italians won that, too.

Masada, I seem to recall, was a miniseries some years or decades back. Like *Exodus,* like *The Diary of Anne Frank,* like *Playing for Time, Schindler's List, Sophie's Choice,* it held the "magic feather." You will remember that Dumbo, the elephant, was taught by Timothy, the mouse, that he could fly if he held the magic feather. The magic feather in film is bathos: the kitten and the dog who must find their way home, the crippled child, Jews dying. *Exodus* bridged the gap. There Jews fight to *stop* dying and to start living. The message, in 1960, contained both the requisite bathos and *novelty.* Today, any potential treatment of the new state contains neither and so is dramatically unacceptable.

But Hollywood never discards the once useful. What, then, shall one do with the Jews? If we, like Ari Ben Canaan, refuse to be victims, perhaps we can be made to serve as villains. Both, we note, identify the subject as "other," and each contains the salutary potential for violence.

The film *The Sum of All Fears* discreetly brings the world to the brink of disaster because the Israelis have thoughtlessly misplaced one of their nuclear bombs. Not only have they forgotten where they put it, they also stole it in the first place, from the U.S.A., which, in the security of its own nuclear programs, was more considerate of the wishes of others.

One might think that this largely narrative off-screen identification of Israelis as villains might be an anomaly, had one not seen it reiterated daily in much of the Western press. (I will make bold to state that some readers of this piece may, in fact, "root" for the Palestinians. I take no issue with their right to that view. I merely state that, irrespective of any reader's assessment of its rectitude, much of the Western press portrays Israelis as monsters.) I will leave the press to chew its own incomprehensible cud and address myself only to the movies.

I predict a growth of the Jew as monster in the next few years' films. Well, why not? Alfonso Bedoya and John Huston inaugurated a few decades of the vicious Mexican ("We don't need no badges! I don't have to show you any stinking badges!"); Jeremy Kemp et al. made the British accent the tocsin of evil quite effectively for quite a while. So I shall naively opine that perhaps turnabout is fair play, and it is merely the Jews' turn in the barrel.

In 1960, Otto Preminger could think of no more magnificent icon than the Israeli officer. Tom Clancy, in a new day, finds them, dramatically, employed better otherwise.

JEWS IN SHOW BUSINESS

These false Jews promote the filth of Hollywood that is seeding
the American people and the people of the world and bringing
you down in moral strength. . . . It's the wicked Jews, the false
Jews . . .

—Louis Farrakhan, 2006

Let me see if I can offend several well-meaning groups at once.
I will address myself particularly to the racially punctilious
and to the goodwilled but otherwise uninvolved champions of
the developmentally challenged: I think it is not impossible
that Asperger's syndrome helped make the movies.

The symptoms of this developmental disorder include early
precocity, a great ability to maintain masses of information, a
lack of ability to mix with groups in age-appropriate ways,
ignorance of or indifference to social norms, high intelligence,
and difficulty with transitions, married to a preternatural ability
to concentrate on the minutia of the task at hand.

This sounds to me like a job description for a movie director. Let me note also that Asperger's syndrome has its highest
prevalence among Ashkenazi Jews and their descendants. For
those who have not been paying attention, this group consti-
tutes, and has constituted since its earliest days, the bulk of
America's movie directors and studio heads.

Neal Gabler, in his *An Empire of Their Own,* points out that the men who made the movies—Goldwyn, Mayer, Schenck, Laemmle, Fox—all came from a circle with Warsaw at its center, its radius a mere two hundred miles. (I will here proudly insert that my four grandparents came from that circle.)

Widening our circle to all of Eastern European Jewry (the Ashkenazim), we find a list of directors beginning with Joe Sternberg's class and continuing strong through Steven Spielberg's and the youth of today.

(A president of Harvard was, in the seventies, defending himself. The admissions policies, theretofore uninterested, started taking cognizance of the place of residence of the applicant. The president called the new program Geographical Diversity or some such and pointed out that in prepolicy, unenlightened days, a statistically anomalous percentage of the student body had come from "the doughnuts surrounding the cities." An alert number of the student body responded, "Those aren't doughnuts, they're bagels.")

As is the movie community.

There was a lot of moosh written in the last two decades about the "blank slate," the idea that since theoretically each child is equal under the law, each must, by extension, be equal in all things and that such a possibility could not obtain unless each child was, from birth, equally capable—environmental influences aside—of succeeding in all things.

This is a magnificent and majestic theory and would be borne out by all save those who had ever had, observed, or seriously thought about children.

Races, as Steven Pinker wrote in his refutational *The Blank Slate,* are just rather large families; families share genes and, thus, genetic dispositions. Such may influence the gene holders (or individuals) much, some, or not at all. The possibility exists, however, that a family passing down the gene for great hand-eye coordination is likely to turn out more athletes than that without. The family possessing the genes for visual acuity will most likely produce good hunters, whose skill will provide nourishment. The families of the good hunters will prosper and intermarry, thus strengthening the genetic disposition in visual acuity.

Among the sons of Ashkenazi families, nothing was more prized than genius at study and explication.

Prodigious students were identified early and nurtured—the gifted child of the poor was adopted by a rich family, which thus gained status and served the community, the religion, and the race.

These boys grew and regularly married into the family or extended family of the wealthy. The precocious ate better, and thus lived longer, and so were more likely to mate and pass on their genes.

These students grew into acclaimed rabbis and Hasidic masters, and founded generations of rabbis; the progeny of these rabbinic courts intermarried, as does any royalty, and that is my amateur Mendelian explication of the prevalence of Asperger's syndrome in the Ashkenazi.

What were the traits indicating the nascent prodigy? Ability to retain and correlate vast amounts of information, a lack of desire (or ability) for normal social interaction, idiosyncrasy, preternatural ability for immersion in minutiae; ecco, six hundred years of Polish rabbis and one hundred of their genetic descendants, American film directors.

Please note that I do not claim for myself and my extended family the *yichus* of descent from the rabbis. My own family history, and, I believe, that of most of the film directors I know (Jewish and otherwise), is firmly that of the ne'er-do-well. I suggest, however, a collateral benefit to the Ashkenazi populace-at-large of the more culturally limited inbreeding of one of its constituent portions.

One does not, of course, have to be Ashkenazi or, indeed, Jewish to succeed as a film director; my genetic divertimento may point out, however, one desideratum of the filmmaker (it need not be hereditary but had better find itself on the CV): experience as a ne'er-do-well.

Proverbs tell us that the stone the builders rejected has become the cornerstone. So it is with anyone in show business, and particularly so of the director. For how could this position, requiring a depraved generalist, attract anyone who had succeeded or was apt to succeed in a specific field?

Just as U. S. Grant failed at everything save preserving the Union, the director is probably one who, by birth, training, or disposition, is gifted and/or driven either to make order out of chaos or to reverse the process.

Loki, Raven, the Fonz, Falstaff, and Larry David are examples of this archetype, the trickster—characters who express or intuit the propensity to upset and so reorder the world on a different level of abstraction, which is the job of moviemaker.

How might one train to tell a story in pictures; assign various crafts and departments their tasks; manage and direct several hundred artists, craftspersons, and administrators; and inspire to meet the exigencies of a grueling production schedule in spite of weather, human nature, chance, et cetera?

It is a job that attracts those who thrive on challenge, chaos, uncertainty, human interaction; who love improvisation; who would rather die than revert to the general population, et cetera—in effect, quasi-criminals.

Note:

1. Yes, there are a lot of Jews in the movie business.
2. No, we did not kill Christ.

THE DEVELOPMENT PROCESS;
OR, LEARNING TO MAKE NOTHING AT ALL!

The artist is, in effect, a sort of gangster. He hitches up his trousers and goes into the guarded bank of the unconscious in an attempt to steal the gold of inspiration. The producer is like the getaway driver who sells the getaway car and waits outside the bank grinning about what a great deal he's made.

There are, admittedly, some good producers. But we must remember that even Diaghilev went into the ballet because he wanted to screw Nijinsky.

What on earth do these producers *do*?

A few are entrepreneurs, raising money for a project under their control; a few are what the shtetl knew as *shtadlans,* that is, intermediaries between the powerless (in this case, the film-maker) and the state (or studio); the rest are clerks or clerk-sycophants.

And we have the sycophants full stop. For the powerful producer, who can drive but one Mercedes himself, can employ or cause to be employed many to drive Their Own Mercedes in his livery.

But some Greek said, or should have said, "If it exists, it probably has a cause."

So let us assume somebody's brother-in-law showed up one day in the palmy presound days of Hollywood, and *his* brother-in-law, a power on the lot or on the set, hoping to avoid a "touch," said, "People, this is Bob, and he is a producer." Bob was then entitled, under the family flag, to all the sex, drugs, and fun he could wrangle and to whatever he could hypothecate.*

Time went by, and Bob stayed on. He, or another of his ilk, caught, stole, or otherwise achieved power in some niche in the industry and, having learned a good trick, one day appointed footmen of his own.

These folk, with nothing much to do, and in the manner of functionaries down through time, schemed all their waking hours to increase and consolidate power.

The filmmakers were busy on the lot or on location, but our producers, like Jacob, stayed in the tents, free to wheedle, convince, and extort position from and in the studio system. Soon all films had a producer, then two, and, today, count 'em, an average of seven in the head titles.

Just as the royalty, another entertainment industry, has keepers of the keys, gentlemen of the bedchamber, and so on, our American charade has coexecutives, executives, and supervising producers ad infinitum.

And, just as with you in your particular racket, our ceremonial positions hide from the uninitiated gaze the empty throne.

And so the producers stay, and live long, why should they not, God bless them. They watch while the lowly make bricks and suggest, at regular intervals, that the brick makers begin to gather their own straw.

---

* The producer's shenanigans were, and are, regulated by unwritten, elastic but generally understood conventions. As such, they are not without precedent. In the Age of Sail, the Bosun was understood to have as his vail or prerequisite a certain extent of the ship's stores. The odd damaged crate, oar, cordage, or spar might be sold over the side, and he might pocket the money. Things being what they are, some, naturally, extended the privilege, endangering the health of the ship, and were fed to the sharks. But we live in a more enlightened time.

And these producers propound heresy.

They sell all parts of the pig but the squeal. And then they sell the squeal.

I have, with my own eyes, seen the following: a sign on the Craft Service (snack) table, near the end of filming: GUM IS FOR PRINCIPAL CAST MEMBERS ONLY.

I have seen the clothing worn by the various cast members auctioned off on eBay, its value increased by the branding of the clothing with the actor's name: "Buy Ricky Jay's pants." "Buy Rebecca Pidgeon's blue jeans." The proceeds go into the producers' purse.

I have seen producers bill the movie salaries for their mistresses, for their absent yes-man, for travel and lodging never used, for services never proffered, for inedible cast and crew meals charged off as gourmet fare, for imaginary bank fees interest, and so on, and so on.

It is one of the staples of talk between actual moviemakers (cast, crew, crafts): "Do you know what that son of a bitch did?" And one comes to tire even of the introduction, "I thought I had seen it all, but . . ." Which is lassitude, indeed.

I've seen, as have we all, theft, fraud, intimidation, malversation, and seen it with such regularity that its absence provokes not comment but wonder.

My favorite offense against the gods, however, is curiously benign and is propounded, usually, not by the savage producer but by the obtuse. To wit:

"We are going about this the wrong way. Why don't we just go in a room, analyze the most successful movies of all time, and then make *that*?"

This, to the filmmaker, is enormity on the order of the resident of wartime Munich suggesting that he thought they were summer camps.

What, the filmmaker wonders, did or do you think we were

doing all of these years, all of these films, whilst you rested in the tents—can you not have seen that we, the filmmakers, were working like mad to solve, film by film, shot by shot, line by line, the problem you suggest a rational person could vanquish by simply "going in a room"?

For this desire to "go in a room" is, to the artist, heresy. It is the reductio ad absurdum of "reality" programming: having determined that it's not necessary to pay either actors or writers, the deluded additionally discover that it is not necessary even to feed the gods—that insight, idiosyncrasy, inspiration, patience, and effort are the concerns of the weak and misguided craftsperson and artist.

No, the exhortation to "go in a room" is not mere crime but blasphemy. It is not sufficient to shake one's head; one must lower the eyes.

The American educational process prepares those with second-rate intellects to thrive in a bureaucratic environment. Obedience, rote memorization, and neatness are enshrined as intellectual achievements. Just as the SAT measures the ability of the applicant to *take that test,* the bureaucratic rigors of the studio system probe the neophyte's threshold for boredom, repetition, sychophancy, and nonsense.

Actual life on the set, where the films are actually being made, is somewhat different.

On the set, a random sampling finds among the workers an actor who won the Academy Award for a short film he wrote, the world's number-two champion arm wrestler, a martial-arts master, a leatherworker, a woodworker, and so on.

The anarchistic nature of a movie set attracts individualists, autodidacts—the interested, the enthused, such as occur only among the truly self-educated.

Eric Hoffer wrote that the mark of a good and healthy society is the ability to function without good leaders. Much work on the set, while apparently hierarchical, is curiously self-directed.

The director in films is an Olympian figure, usually removed from the life of the set, his wishes or whims relayed to the workers by functionaries. In television the post seems largely ceremonial—the film *is* going to get in the can. (The ancient television phrase has it: features in the morning, documentaries in the afternoon.) How does the film get into the can?

The ostensibly hierarchical arrangement—director, department head, worker—is a chain of information that relies for execution on the man or woman on the set. The necessity for improvisation is so great that the strictly hierarchical worker could not and cannot survive. The directions given may be more or less succinct, but the possibility of their execution will almost always require intuition, improvisation—in short, art.

The art of the worker has been of the essence in the *artistic* success of films: Zoltan Korda's painted shadows in the boat-deck scene between Mary Astor and Walter Huston in *Dodsworth,* Ken Adam's code machine in the B-52 in *Dr. Strangelove,* the skill of the grips moving the dolly in the calliope shot in *The Rules of the Game,* the timing of the thrown snow in W. C. Fields's *The Fatal Glass of Beer.*

The variety and flat-out humor, the sordid tragedy, the perversity of human existence are explorable only by those experiencing them: the artists and the workers.

On the other hand, the young bureaucrat-in-training, as he progresses in the bureaucratic hierarchy, will discover—some quickly; others, their eventual lackeys, with less speed—that success comes not from pleasing the audience but from placating his superiors until that time it is reasoned effective to betray them.

He learns, in short, to bide his time.

And as time goes by, this suborned young person becomes

each day less capable of first uttering and then framing a non-bureaucratic thought.

Impulses of joy, of wonder, indeed, of rage and grief are repressed until they are no longer consciously felt.

This is called "growing savvy."

This person, like a member of a sexless marriage, ceases to feel affection, lust, desire for the permitted object, and, as in that marriage, this energy is diverted into (inter alia) depression, abuse, and treachery.

The successfully matriculated executive, marginally concerned with art and diminishingly concerned even with "product," devotes his new wisdom and increased leisure to opportunities for trickery, greed, stock manipulation, and merger, as in any business.

In the film business, one department of this glee is called "the development process."

This is the fig leaf of propriety covering, if I may, not the genitals of artistic potential but the empty space where they once lay.

Karen Horney wrote of a neurotic who could never complete anything. She was impeded now by this, now by that mischance and was eternally blighted and blocked, just on the edge of the creation of a great work. Ever saddened but still valiant, she pressed on, content in her own untested but undoubted abilities.

On completion, any creation is torn from the prospective fantasy of creative potential and consigned to the world, there to brave and bear the opinion not only of others but also of its creator.

But not the film in development.

This film need never cross that divide.

This project is, in fact, a film only by courtesy.

It functions, as do the endless and proliferating committees of Government, as a repository of bureaucratic power. This power exists, and can exist, only in *potential*—for should the committee ever come to conclusions, its task, and so its operation as a bureaucratic fiefdom, would cease. So the bureaucrat, studio or otherwise, learns not only of the inadvisability of any test or completion but also of such conclusions' absolute foolishness.

This lesson, we see, was learned very well by the folks at Enron et al.—executives who saw that the power to grow wealthy stemmed from the brave decision to stop making anything at all.

THE REPRESSIVE MECHANISM

A DARK COMEDY

America is a self-created society.

That a self-created group could rule itself, absent religious or hereditary oversight, subject only to the dictates of reason, is all very well. The body politic, however, constantly strives to re-create for itself that same irrational, repressive (that is, effective) governing authority otherwise vested in tradition, popes, and kings.

Such authority may be called patriotism and, as such, may helpfully identify convenient enemies foreign and domestic; or we may create a civil version of religion and call it "family values," liberalism, Americanism, or the American way. We may, also, uniquely in history, name this ad hoc authority "entertainment."

The absence of a historical and universally acknowledged authority to which one may pledge fealty and against which one may rebel creates factionalism: the right moves toward fascism, the left toward chaos. Democracy—in extremis— seems capable of devolving to either tyranny or civil war, and America, maddened by unimaginable prosperity and safety, incomprehensibly powerful, and bereft of threats, splits down the middle on the issue of *definition*.

Is the good person one who will not tolerate a president's lies about sex or one who will not tolerate a president's lies about war? Neither of these outrages is without precedent, but the country, in its anomie of wealth and faced with the unbearable reality of its own self-government, is reduced to what is essentially a neurosis. That is, "I know something is wrong, but I cannot identify it." The resulting free-floating anxiety is exchanged, in a good trade, for an obsession—in this case, the search for an internal enemy.

Two basic strategies, per party, are: on the right, "people are swine—endorse my position, or join them in my estimation"; and on the left, "people are basically good at heart, can't you see that, you sick fool?" One strategy to combat in the awkward burden of democracy is the establishment of aristocracies: the Kennedys, the Bushes, Frank Sinatra Jr., et al. This, of course, never answers, for the palace, the manufactory, the final clubs of Harvard, and the stage have bequeathed us little other than attenuated genes.

The continent was paved and wired by the common people free of authority; now, as we lift our heads from our labors or our depredations, the absence of authority is driving us mad. (How, we wonder, could that which was won by unchecked aggression be held by any other strategies—must not those similarly avaricious see in us that same rich continent, ripe for plunder, which our forefathers saw?) In effect, the miser cannot sleep. And in our madness, we have pressed entertainment, which is to say tincture of art, into the service of the repressive mechanism.

In the 1960s, philosophers of communications observed that television viewers sometimes did not laugh at gags that, in the studio, seemed quite hilarious. Those scientists opined that the home viewer was inhibited by the absence of the herd—that the individual, all alone, may sit unmoved at the same jokes that would convulse a full auditorium; that there was ineluctably something of the *communal* in the impulse of laughter, the viewer delighting not only in the *gag* but also in sharing with his like the notion, "Isn't life like that?"

Home viewers, then, who would not laugh alone, were freed from their inertia by the addition of the laugh track. It was later noted, however, that given this effective tool, the quality of the joke itself became moot.

One sees this brave aperçu applied in the pronouncements of our contemporary government. Periodic declarations assuage fully half of the populace absent any correspondence between that verbiage and the government's actions or, indeed, between them and the plausible. The administration, like the sitcom of old, has discovered that, given an immobilized audience, a presentation of the form itself is sufficient entertainment.

Big and bad films, summer films, blockbusters have similarly become the laugh track to our national experiment. As with the Defense Department, we are reassured by their presence rather than their content or operations. As examples of waste they appeal to our need—not for entertainment but for security.

The very vacuousness of these films is reassuring, for they ratify for the viewer the presence of a repressive mechanism and offer momentary reprieve from anxiety with this thought: "Enough money spent can cure anything. You are a member of a country, a part of a system capable of wasting two hundred million dollars on an hour and a half of garbage. You must be *somebody*."

The same mechanism operates equally in the Defense Department.

"Soft on defense" is a war cry directed not against the country's enemies but at those who are soft on defense; the right understands (consciously or unconsciously) that a conveniently frightened populace wants security and that not *defense* but *defense spending* absolutely (if momentarily) supplies it.

This addiction is conveniently both self-ratifying and self-perpetuating, for if the country is *not* at risk after spending, the spending, now proved effective, must, logically, be continued. And if the country is *still* at risk after increased spending, the only cure must be further expenditure.

As with defense, the paradigm in blockbuster entertainment is "more will cure it." But the natural desire for true entertainment can be fulfilled only by the truly entertaining. The truly entertained audience member leaves the theater chuckling or shaking his head sagely—in either case, *fulfilled*. Those, on the other hand, who have been treated to an outing of *waste* are reenrolled in the service of the repressive mechanism, have experienced no fulfillment, and are driven to increase their expenditure and repeat their error. (Vide the hypnotized televiewer glued for five irreplaceable hours each evening in front of the set.)

The winning gambler slogs back, soon or late, into the casino, for he craves not riches but, *ultimately,* the thrill offered by his addiction. He returns to the toxic environment and its whore's promise of joy, driven mad by his own irrational actions. He tells himself he plays to win, but when he wins, he plays until he loses and, losing, plays in an effort to restore his winnings.

For America to engage in pointless, destructive, irrational foreign enterprise is, essentially, for the electorate to endorse a bad, empty, addictive entertainment.

Perhaps the success of Michael Moore's film *Fahrenheit 9/11* is due to its excellence not as a documentary but as a *comedy*. A comedy is the form in which the unsayable is said and that, thus, for a moment, breaks the corrosive cycle of repression.

AN AMERICAN TRAGEDY

My title refers not to the 1931 film with Phillips Holmes and Sylvia Sidney, nor to the story's treatment as *A Place in the Sun* (1951), nor to Dreiser's 1925 novel on which the two are based, but to another quintessential American film document, *The Jolson Story*.

This 1946 film is a pretty good musical, and musical document, of the career of Al Jolson, who started out as a busker in saloons and ended as one of the first media superstars on stage, on the radio, and in motion pictures.

The film and its attendant meditation also offer a good clinical study of American confusion.

A. J. Liebling wrote of two boxers in the ring "working out their tight little problem." That is what we have here. And the tight little problem is race. Young Asa Yoelson is the son of a cantor. We see him first singing the liturgy in shul, but he discovers vaudeville and wants to get into show business. His straightlaced and religious father forbids it. So Asa runs away. He is caught by the cops and taken for safekeeping to a Catholic church. When his dad, the cantor, catches up with him, Asa has been pressed into the choir and is singing a solo in "Ave Maria." His father, the cantor, duly impressed by that talent that can be revealed only through ecumenicism, relents, and the son goes into show business.

He leaves the shul, he leaves his home, he changes his name to Al Jolson, and there you go.

Now this newcomer pines for a break, as one does, and one night, Tom Baron, a blackface performer, gets drunk and can't go on. Al puts him to bed, blacks up, and does his act. Great impresarios are, by chance, in the audience, and Al's talent is recognized.

Not to put too fine a point upon it, but Al, a poor Jewish immigrant kid, gets his first break from impersonating a Christian (the European solution) and his second from impersonating a black man (the more American choice). He is now on his way, taken up by Lew Dockstader of Dockstader's Minstrels. These minstrels, an American tradition, are white performers in blackface, presenting a traditional evening of "darky" songs.

Al's job, for three years, is to sing, "I want a girl just like the girl who married dear old Dad." This work is steady but other than rewarding. And then one night in New Orleans, he wanders, musing and unquiet, into Storyville and hears jazz. His life is changed. He quits the minstrels and retires in meditation to reinvent himself.

As one might, at this point, he returns home. His family has not seen him for three years. He explains he is on the track of something new—he wants to bring jazz, black music, to the world at large—that is, to the white world.

Now let us become psychoanalytical. He is ushered to the family table; he sits, ready to eat; and his mother sneaks him a yarmulke. He is a Jew, his father is a member of the clergy; they are, of course, observant; one cannot eat without first blessing the meal; and a man cannot say the blessing with an uncovered head. He puts on the yarmulke, and his canny father says "Asa, did you wear the cap while you were on the road?" "No," he responds sheepishly. "Not all the time."

"Well, then," says his father, "you don't have to wear the cap for me. . . ."

Who ever referred to a yarmulke as a "cap"? Whose feelings are being spared, whose lack of intellect is being considered, in referring to a yarmulke as a cap?

Further, why would his father, a cantor, endorse (accept, perhaps, but not endorse) Al's irreligious behavior?

But he does, and all are happy to have reached this particularly American détente—or repression as the cost of assimilation—at which exact point the phone rings.

Now, in psychoanalysis, there is no such thing as accident, no such thing as coincidence or mere happenstance. Neither is there in dramaturgy. The phone rings *because* Al has set aside his race and religion.

And who is on the phone? It is, of course, Tom Baron, now a successful theater manager, offering Al a slot in a new and important Broadway show.

Yes, Al says, of course I will do it. But I have to sing "this new music"? Well, okay.

Opening night at the Winter Garden, Al is due to do a solo, but the show is running late, and Oscar Hammerstein tells the stage manager to bring down the curtain before Al's turn. Al rushes onstage and demands the orchestra play his song. The song is "Mammy," and Al brings down the house, and his career is assured. He becomes a cultural icon.

He stars in the first talking picture, *The Jazz Singer,* 1927.

In it he plays a nice Jewish boy, son of a cantor, who runs away from home to join show business. In the film's climactic moment, the cantor becomes ill, and the boy must forsake his Broadway show to rush back to the shul and sing Kol Nidre.

The lead in our film, *The Jolson Story,* is played by Larry Parks.

This is one of the most remarkable performances I've

ever seen on film. Parks lip-synchs some twenty Jolson songs, *inhabiting* them. The voice is actually Al Jolson's, the fervor, the grace, and humor are Parks's in a spectacular display of commitment, love, and skill.

What a beginning to a career. Parks went on to repeat his success in the sequel *Jolson Sings Again* and thence to the ministrations of the House Un-American Activities Committee (1951), which pilloried him for membership in the American Communist Party, at which point he was blacklisted and run out of show business. The McCarthy era ran quite a bit of the show business out of show business, and we were left with *Pillow Talk.*

But the America films, *the* mass medium, have always, and lovingly, expressed ethnocentrism. Vide Robert Alda helping Louis Armstrong and Billie Holiday to find the true meaning of jazz in *New Orleans* (1947); *Dances With Wolves,* in which Kevin Costner teaches the Lakota Sioux to hunt buffalo; *Homo sapiens'* Rae Dawn Chong in *Quest for Fire* (1981), bringing the benefits of the missionary position to the Neanderthals.

For in American film the whites teach the blacks to play jazz; Gregory Peck, a Christian, impersonates a Jew (*Gentleman's Agreement,* 1947) and lectures his Jewish secretary on her lack of racial pride; Oskar Schindler, a Christian, saves the Jews, as, in myriad films of the Pacific war, strapping GIs teach their little brown brothers, the Filipinos, how to defeat the Japs.

A tight little problem.

Samson Raphaelson wrote *The Jazz Singer.* I wrote my first screenplay, *The Postman Always Rings Twice,* for his nephew, Bob Rafelson. One day, during a script conference, Bob's uncle called, and Bob put him on the line, and Sam gave me notes on my screenplay. I thought his notes quite wrong, and I was right to think it. For who rides, decides.

One needs a vast amount of self-confidence to make movies.

When wrong-footed by a recalcitrant audience or, indeed, by time, this decisiveness is known as arrogance.

But which of us knows his time, and how many lunatic or vile creations of our day are labeled good clean fun?

Is it the place of films to address social issues, or are they merely *son et lumière,* signifying nothing?

So we see *The Jolson Story.* It is a fascinating document, a stunning performance by the subsequent nonperson, Parks, and the great singing of Jolie himself. Note also a long shot during the number "Swanee," in which, I believe, it is Jolson himself, onstage, doing a buck-and-wing.

AN UNDERSTANDING AND
A MISUNDERSTANDING OF
THE REPRESSIVE MECHANISM

I once did an action picture. One sequence was supposed to take place on a rooftop in Dubai. It was shot on a rooftop in Los Angeles. The Dubai background was added by a computer. The computer background was as real, photographically, as the actors in the foreground, but the composite shot, to me, always looked false. After the film was released, it occurred to me: the foreground and the background could not *both* be in focus. Whether or not the viewer was aware of this consciously, the shot, to the unconscious, *had* to look wrong.

(I gained this insight from watching some excellent feature cartoons, or animated features, as I believe they are now called. Some brilliant animators have begun to throw the background out of focus, mimicking film.)

The movie business humbles the overly theoretical financially as well.

Every studio pays myriads of number crunchers, market analysts, and various other experts to predict and strategize. The breakaway hits, however, have usually been films that were originally discarded as "too."

"Too" what? What matter? Too original, too predictable, too mature, too infantile, too genre, not sufficiently genre, et cetera.

Harry Cohn famously commented that he knew when a

film was doing well by the feeling in his ass. I'm with him. For, finally, the decision to green-light a film or to pass on it is made by some man or woman who is sitting where the buck stops and guessing.

Napoléon frowned on councils of war, as he vowed never "to take counsel of his fears."

Executives, coming now as they do in the main from the ranks of businesspeople rather than show people, have never had the opportunity to learn how to rely on their instincts. So the film business is currently plagued by audience research.

What is wrong with audience research? It doesn't work. *If* it worked, there would be no flops.

But wait—is it not common sense to ask a potential viewer if she would see such-and-such a film, to ask a preview viewer what he would like to change? It may be common sense, but it is useless. Why?

Consider the difference between the barbershop and the jury room.

In the barbershop, beauty parlor, subway, and so on, we gossip. There is much enjoyment in knowing better than the principals, in realizing the error of the prosecution, the defense, the Defense Department, the indicted captains of industry and their mouthpieces. We form and express our vehement opinions based on information that is incomplete and, most probably, skewed or, indeed, manufactured.

Why not? That is the purpose and the joy of gossip—to strengthen community norms through essentially dramatic discourse.

In the jury room, however, we are sworn. We struggle, individually and as a group, to put *aside* prejudice, to put aside the pleasures of gossip, the proxy exercise of power, vicarious revenge, et cetera, and to act according to a set of rules.

The jury is continually taught and admonished to use

reason, as the stakes—the fate or condition of another human being—demand it.

In audience testing, the situation is reversed. Appreciation of drama, an endeavor that has been *correctly* and *necessarily* consecrated to a form of gossip, has been degraded into a mock trial. The tester insists that we put aside our *not only personal but also necessarily inchoate* reactions to a drama and apply an idealized norm of human behavior.

This norm is idealized both in the projection of a putative imaginary viewer (over whom we are to exercise responsible control) and in our self-idealization. For the questioned viewer asks himself not only "Is this the sort of movie I like?" and "Is this the sort of movie 'someone like me' might like?" but also, most corrosively, "Is this the sort of movie someone like me would *proclaim* to like?"

At this point any subjective experience of the film is banished by reason. What remains? The power to teach or admonish—both of which are death to any art.

The filmgoer has been turned into Babbitt, responsible for the film rather than a member of the audience. As a newly responsible member of a jury he will, of course, take the safest course.

What is the safest course? To rationally exclude that which may not be explained. This is much the wisest course for the surveyed, which is why the executive has enlisted him. His refusal to be moved by a film, his characterization of the disturbing or unusual as anathema, has relieved from the troubled mind of the studio bureaucrat the responsibility of *taste,* which is to say, of *choice.*

To succeed, a film must treat the audience member *as* an audience member, not as a commissar of culture. The commissar gets her thrill not from the film but from the power to admonish. (That's why moviegoers fill out the cards after a screening, engaging in a process that would be recognized as an imposition were it not for the honor of the thing.)

But the real filmmakers have to listen to the lessons of their ass.

Will they fail? Certainly. Both artistically and commercially. But (a) they have no other choice and (b) *realizing* that their final choices must be essentially subjective, they may learn to trust their instincts. Also (c) they'll have more fun.

Is it not necessary to gauge the audience? Sure thing. The way to do it is to sit in the back of the theater while the film is being screened and watch their reactions *when their attention is off themselves;* that's the way to see if the film, and any section of it, works or fails.

For that is the state the eventual viewer of the films will be in: disbelief suspended, attention on the screen—wanting to be thrilled, pleased, and diverted, hoping along with the hero, and fearing the villain; and to lead the moviegoer to that state, one cannot ask for his opinion but must pay attention to his actions.

CORRUPTION

Must all human conglomerations become corrupt? Past a certain point they seem to—that point beyond which each person in the group no longer knows the names of all the others.

It requires a genius of morality—in effect, a hero—to remain pure while involved in the conflicting rewards and temptations of power, to avoid arrogance and despair in the face of human corruptibility.

Many movie stars, directors, and producers exhibit the manners, literally, of a two-year-old—a being imagining itself to have vast power, and ignorant of responsibility, enraged by the least human noncompliance as with the broken top that refuses to spin.

The stock-in-trade, however, of the moviemaker, and, most especially, of the actor, is to show how the hero behaves in extremity—fear, greed, lust, hatred, injustice—and to inspire a like stoicism: to show the hero's valiant effort to overcome internal and external evil, to embody the villain's simple conviction of his own rectitude, and, therefore, to inculcate in the viewer a horror of sin.

Perhaps the greatest dramatic portrayal in film is Vittorio De Sica in *General della Rovere*.

Roberto Rossellini's 1959 film has De Sica as a confidence man in wartime Naples. He makes his living bilking the families of those detained by the Nazis. He sells false hope of his influence and uses his stolen gains to gamble.

His simple, kind, and completely believable appeals to his victims are terrifying. He is a monster without shame who justifies all his depredations, who sees extenuation for his incalculable viciousness. Much like you and me.

A Nazi colonel discovers him and offers a bargain. He may go free if he agrees to spy on the Partisans.

The Partisans' General della Rovere has been snuck into Italy to oppose the Nazis. He was to have made contact with the extant Partisan cell in Naples; he has, however, been shot by a Nazi sentry. The Partisans are unaware of his death. One of their cells has been apprehended. The Nazi colonel needs to know which one is the Partisan leader, and he asks De Sica to impersonate General della Rovere to gain the confidence of the group and to determine the identity of its head. In return, De Sica will go free.

De Sica, as the general, is greeted in prison with limitless respect. He hears of "his" wife, returning from safety in Switzerland to see him once more before he dies; he sees a prison mate tortured to death rather than reveal names. The colonel presses him to find out who is the head of the group. De Sica is reluctant.

Finally, the colonel sentences the entire group to death. In the long night before the execution, the head of the Partisan group reveals himself to De Sica.

In the morning, the Nazi colonel asks De Sica one last time: reveal the name, which it is now evident you know, and go free. De Sica refuses. He pens a note of courage to his (General della Rovere's) wife, he exhorts his fellow condemned to courage, and he is shot.

A thoroughly bad man has been humbled sufficiently to choose death rather than deny the voice of God.

It is a magnificent story—and portrayal—of martyrdom. One leaves the film wanting to kill not the Jews but the evil in oneself. One is humbled, as was De Sica's character, by the very distance he had fallen from good and by the extraordinary, miraculous power of awakened consciousness. Having sunk lower than imaginable in disgrace, he is given the opportunity and chooses grace and glory for himself, and we, the audience, are moved and strengthened by his sacrifice.

Movies are a potentially great art. Like any human endeavor, like you and me, they have inevitably been exposed to and have, in the main, submitted to the power of self-corruption, of self-righteousness, to the abuse of power. But like General della Rovere, like you and me, like the studio executives, they possess the possibility of beauty and, hence, for human transformation: not as preaching, not as instruction, not as doctrine—all of which, finally, are out of place in the cinema and can awaken, at best, but self-righteousness. Movies possess the power to speak to the human soul, to free us from the weight of repression.

What is repressed? Our knowledge of our own worthlessness.

The truth cleanses, but the truth hurts—everywhere but in the drama, where, in comedy or tragedy, the truth restores through art.

The audience has a right to these dramas, and the filmmaker and the studios have a responsibility to attempt them.

THE SCREENPLAY

HOW TO WRITE A SCREENPLAY

As an American occupation, screenwriting has replaced knitting which it, in some ways, resembles: the rules for both are simple, and both involve sheep.

—Richard Weisz

An expert in probability calculated that the odds against winning the lottery are so high that one does not appreciably lower them by neglecting to buy a ticket.

One might, he wrote, stand an equal chance of success by occasionally casting one's glance at the ground in hope of finding that winning ticket some careless soul had dropped.

So it is with the writing of the screenplay.

So many are written, so few are made, and the majority of those are written by that tiny coterie of Mamelukes, harem detainees, or house slaves who constitute the chosen among the Hollywood faithful.

These fattened cattle, myself included, are preserved not to write but to provide the unwary starry-eyed aspirants a further goad to their unpaid efforts.

This is the American way at its finest, which is to say, most operational, pitch—that one, if dedicated, hardworking, vicious, and blind to the blandishments of conscience, common sense, or good taste, might, through chance and/or devotion, rise to that pinnacle where he was licensed to oppress the latecomers.

We have spoken of chance.

What of devotion?

To what rule or force might one devote oneself to ensure success as a screenwriter?

Schools and individual buccaneers spring up to instruct the gullible and hopeful: "Learn the Secrets of the Second Act," "Learn How to Harness the Secret Power of Chaos," "Earn an MFA in Screenwriting."

These educational entities appeal to the common sense of the ignorant.

That is, they present a syllogism that is inherently logical.

It is, however, false.

One can study marching, the entry-level skill of the military, until one shines at it as has none other. This will not, however, make it more likely that one will be tapped to be the Secretary of the Army.

But the *true* entry-level skill of the scenarist, he discovers, is not blind obedience to authority but loathing and distrust of the same. For if the Authority—the agencies, the studios, the producers—knew what they were doing, they would all be peaceful, content, happy, and benevolent instead of caught in a constant, never-abating struggle to the knife.

What are these folks struggling for? For power.

Where does the power come from? From money, access to same, and access to material (scripts) and to stars.

One gains access to stars either through having been both poor and honest with them or through having made them money.

One gains access to money through having been poor and dishonest along with fellow producers or agents.

But *anyone* can gain access to a script. Because anyone can *write* a script.

Just as the young and sexually vulnerable present them-selves in these western precincts as victims, so the mantra of the neophyte screenwriter is: I am young and stupid. Please abuse me.

Let us consider the screeenwriter's process structurally, as the drama that it is.

Act 1:

These just-off-the-bus newcomers arrive enthused—as is the way of the young—with the idea that they are the first to have had the idea.

The idea is: There is nothing I will not do to get ahead.

Oh, really.

But just as with the fresh-faced bimbo or gigolo in bed, there are, finally, only so many things the acolyte screenwriter can *do*:

He can do exactly as he is told, which puts him in the same applicant pool as everyone else who just got off the bus, or he can break new ground.

But the ersatz producers, the bottom feeders who hound the bus station looking for prey, are not interested in breaking new ground with film. They are not interested in film at all. They have no time. They are, like the other bus riders, pos-sessed only with the big idea—in their case: I will take your something for nothing and sell it to my betters. For as Neal Stephenson informed us, Hollywood is just a bank.

These ersatz producers have no dramatic sense, which would, had they possessed it, nix whatever chance they might have of putting the focaccia on the table—they observe that which has been successful and attempt to duplicate it. They want, in effect, to find the script for the hit of last year.

But—and here's the twist—in the *new* script, instead of being a cod, it will be a mackerel.

Yes, yes, yes, say these entrepreneurs—yes. A mackerel. Great, let me run with it.

Now we have act 2. My, what will happen? Oh no. The producer is returning to the starry-eyed, unpaid, and biddable screenwriter. Can it be good news?

Well, it could be worse, the producer reports: I, or my advisors, or that big independent money person (that gunrunning, drug money launderer) from (fill in the country) with whom I have been talking, am interested in your script: I just want you to do one thing.

Could the mackerel live in a tank in a restaurant rather than in the Indian Ocean?

Why not, one responds, what a *great* idea, thank you for the suggestion.

As this act progresses, we see the producer coming back to the writer with more and more "ideas" from his real and imaginary sources, supporters, and advisors:

Instead of a restaurant, could it be Mars, and instead of a mackerel, could it be Woodrow Wilson, et cetera.

And now what happens?

Just as he does with the nubile offerings of fresh young things, the producer gets tired of being offered "anything you want."

"Jeez," he thinks, "doesn't this person have any self-respect? I am ashamed to *know* someone who would stoop to such degrady." And the producer moves on.

Here, the producer, about to decamp, realizes that the writer brings him nothing special, that if the *writer* doesn't know good from bad, and is endlessly biddable, how can the producer trust him. He cannot.

The now-mangled script has become the fruit of the poison tree and must be discarded as unclean. Which it is. And the producer moves on in the hope that *one* of these free scripts just might, magically, attract the favorable notice of someone with a bit more power.

Let us suppose that the screenwriter has, over a period of time, paid his dues (i.e., been seduced and abandoned sufficiently to tire of it).

Here, at, as we say, the break of act 3, the sadder-but-wiser screenwriter is free to examine the tropism that got him into this mess in the first place. Why, oh why, he muses, did I come to Hollywood? To write screenplays/to find success as a screenwriter/to have an adventure.

Well, one may *still* write screenplays.

In many arts, we are told, the proselyte presents himself as food for the gods, a sacrifice of pleasing odor, saying, "Bid me."

We know of the young dancer, athlete, musician, martial artist who wants no reward greater or other than the opportunity to serve the muse. So, then, to the abused and failed immigrant, should that be your happy desire, what hinders you?

What, however, if one still craves success?

In that case, perhaps the protagonist possesses sufficient honesty to avow that his efforts to "be just like everybody else, except *more so*" have not availed and that the bloom is off the rose. Perhaps a healthy self-evaluation would lead to the conclusion that one, in fact, finds the perpetual abuse degrading and that no possible success is worth the shame and rejection. Perhaps one harbors the residual belief that learning to write a screenplay "better" might improve one's chances of selling it. I don't think so. I, however, sadly harbor the same delusion, so as a continuation of the abuse you have already taken, I will end my play on an inconclusive note (the writer's suicide is too easy—his return to a cabin in Vermont unbelievable) and tell you my advice on the subject of screenwriting.

CHARACTER, PLOT, DIALOGUE,
CAMERA ANGLES, ADVICE TO THE EDITOR

Let's examine a perfect movie: *The Lady Eve,* written and directed by Preston Sturges.

His work is, to me, irrefutable proof of an afterlife, for it is impossible to make films that sweet and not go to heaven.

Here we have Barbara Stanwyck and her father, Charles Coburn. They are cardsharps and confidence tricksters plying the liners.

Here comes Henry Fonda, an amateur naturalist and the filthy rich son of Eugene Palette. He's been up the Amazon for a year and is going home.

Everyone on the liner is angling for his notice or favor. Stanwyck, of course, wins out. And she and her father set out to fell Fonda.

This is called a premise.

Stanwyck, however, makes the mistake of actually falling in love with him.

This is called a complication.

Her love is reciprocated, and Fonda proposes marriage.

But wait—before she can accept, she must confess to her past life of sin, and before she gets to do so, the ship's purser warns Fonda that she is a criminal.

He is heartbroken and tells her that he knew it all along and was just stringing her along for the entertainment value. She, now, is also heartbroken.

And now we have Billy Wilder's famous dictum posed as a Talmudic question, in re love stories: *What keeps them apart?*

Aha. The lovers are now kept apart by loathing on the part of Fonda and, upon the part of Stanwyck, by a desire for revenge.

Enter act 2.

She decides to impersonate a wealthy British countess or something, get introduced into Fonda's family's rich Connecticut set, and win him *all over again*.

She, of course, does so, and they get married.

We now have act 3. They are together, but the notional forces have not been propitiated. He has been won not through love but through actual chicanery (the very method she disdained in act 1), and Stanwyck must have her revenge.

They proceed on their honeymoon. About to consummate the marriage, she confesses first to one and then to a very lengthy run of sexual encounters, and he dumps her.

She has had her revenge, his family proposes a fat settlement, and she turns it down. All she wants is for her husband to ask outright for his release.

Note, she has won both her prize of the first act (money) and that of the second (regard) but finds that revenge is empty—that she has, in fact, gone too far. She has heaped Ossa on Pelion and now has nothing.

Fonda, she learns, is going back down the Amazon.

In a fit of inspiration, she boards his boat in her old persona as the rejected con artist.

He is overjoyed to meet her again and calls her to his bosom. Great story. And we may reflect that its description contains none of what the ignorant refer to as "characterization," nor does it contain any of their beloved "backstory."

These, and the attendant filth of authorial narrative (he comes in the room, and we see that the place to which he's going is going to be far more interesting than the place to which he's been), are the screenwriting equivalent of HIV: they spread like mad, they corrupt everything they touch, and there is no known cure.

A director could (indeed, did) *shoot* the story above. It was simple and straightforward enough to allow him to make simple choices about clothes, costumes, camera angles, music, and so on.

Actors could *act* upon those directions he gave them based upon the script.

The resultant film, though made by a master, would probably have been watchable if made by a journeyman. Why? Because we, the audience (those in their seats at the cinema and you, gentle reader, no less), wanted to know what happened next. That is more or less the total art of the film dramatist: to make the audience want to know what is going to happen next.

The garbage of exposition, backstory, narrative, and characterization spot-welds the reader into interest in what is happening *now*. It literally stops the show.

A wiser man than I might advise you, gentle reader, to write— if you must write, and if you must write for Hollywood—*two* scripts: one to appeal to those who man the conference rooms of the Valley; the other, once you've obtained their imprimatur, an actual document capable of being designed, filmed, and acted.

I can't do so. For it is one thing to take candy from a baby, another to take candy from a baby and give the baby typhus, and this two-scripts idea (though practicable in the extreme) is, to me, a heresy.

Samson (from the Hebrew for *sun*) eventually gives in to Delilah (from the Aramaic for *night*) 'cause he just can't stand her noodging.

He winds up eyeless in Gaza, and we all might just take a lesson from it. He got what he wanted (a little nookie), and he overpaid for it.

One may similarly manipulate the story, but the deviation from the essential—what does the hero want, what prevents him from getting it?—renders the writer no different from, indeed, an adjunct (read: whore) to, the forces of commoditization.

But wait, but wait, are not these the very forces one is trying to propitiate?

Perhaps, but that pursuit is not the task of screenwriting, in which case this chapter will be of no avail.

Where did we leave our burden?

We had crafted a plot reducible to five lines on one side of one sheet of paper.

It begins with a premise: the hero wants something. His desire begins with the *beginning of the film.*

That is, he cannot *just* desire something. For the screenplay to be coherent and compelling, his desire must be awakened by a new circumstance. That circumstance is the film.

Barbara Stanwyck meets the love of her life, Henry Fonda. The film starts *because* she meets him. The progress of the film is her progress toward attainment of her goal. When she attains it (in the last ten seconds), the film, the story, is over.

Each act of the film must concern her progress toward that goal and the complications thereof.

Act 1, she wants to win his money.

Act 2, she wants revenge.

Act 3, she wants reconciliation.

Each scene, act per act, is her attempt to win from the antagonist (Fonda) the special prize that, *in that act,* signifies her possession of him: money, reconciliation, love. Then, there you go, screenwriter. You are now all set. Write down your premise, tell yourself the story act by act. The small steps in each act are called scenes.

Now write each scene such that it is essential to the hero's progress toward the goal of that act.

In order to win Fonda's money, Barbara Stanwyck must first get his attention. She trips him. He breaks the heel off her shoe. To consolidate her gain (his attention), she makes him schlep her down to her cabin to find a new pair of heels.

The act culminates as she realizes that she wants to possess not his money but his love; simultaneously, he discovers she is a con woman and insults her.

Which leads us to act 2, Revenge.

What could be simpler?

And that's how one writes a screenplay.

"Cinema, at its most effective, is one scene effectively superseded by the next. Isn't that it?" (George Stevens, 1973).

I don't think he left anything out.

HELPFUL HINTS ON SCREENWRITING

> "A guy comes home from college to find his mother sleeping with his uncle, and there's a ghost running around. Write it good, it's *Hamlet;* write it bad, it's *Gilligan's Island.*"
>
> —Lorne Michaels

The audience will undergo only that journey that the hero undergoes.

Similarly, the audience will not suffer, wonder, discover, or rejoice to any extent greater than that to which the writer has been subjected. To suggest that the writer can, through exercise of craft, evade or avoid the struggle of creation is an error congruent with confounding the study of theology with prayer.

In what could a graduate course in screenwriting consist?

There are two possibilities.

It may, perhaps, instruct in first principles (i.e., it may consist of the study of that branch of philosophy called aesthetics). These first principles were best enumerated by Aristotle in his *Poetics* (a dissection of *Oedipus Rex*), and they are famously few: unity of time, place, and action.

That is: the story should come to life before our eyes—brought into being by a unique event, as opposed to an "ongoing process" (e.g., the hero should want to raise the plague on Thebes, rather than discover the cause of evil in the world). This story should take place within the space of three days, in one place, and should consist *solely* of the attempt of the hero to solve the problem whose appearance gave rise to the play. That's it.

And like the Gospels or the Torah, child rearing, or marriage, anyone truly interested can and will have to figure out the rest.

To correctly *formulate the problem,* specifically and mechanically, and then to work out the solution (the steps the hero must undergo) is a daunting process. It calls for perseverance, honesty, and, by turns, blunt candor, invention, humor, and humility. The process is made more difficult by the opportunities for chicanery.

Faced with the dead end of the first act, the author may, in fact, revert to the formulaic. He may, in effect, forge a corrupt bond with the audience—i.e., "You and I know that, at this point, a change must take place. That the barn catches fire will serve as notice that, though I, the author, have not solved the problem, I at least recognize your, the audience's, right to a solution." It is laudable to resist this nagging invitation to sloth and predictability.

(Most studio notes on a script or a film are an insistence that the intrinsically inevitable, thought-out, and, so, surprising turns of the script be junked in favor of the formulaic.)

Again, the rules of dramaturgy are few, their application difficult, their product unusual, idiosyncratic, and surprising—that is to say, dramatic.

Are there other books one might read to better understand these simple precepts?

There are. I would name *The Uses of Enchantment* by Bruno Bettelheim, *The Hero with a Thousand Faces* by Joseph Campbell, and my own *Three Uses of the Knife.*

Those bitten by a love of the form will, of course, discover a vast assortment of texts and might, if truly enthused, ponder the psychological or, indeed, the neurological nature that gave rise to the human longing for drama.

Raymond and Lorna Coppinger, in their wonderful book *Dogs* (2001), argue that, in a Darwinian sense, the various breeds indulge in breed-specific behavior *not* to achieve a (causally related) end but because the behavior in itself is enjoyable.

They cite the sled dog, which, in their decades-long experience as sled-dog racers, runs, they have found, not through fear of the driver's whip (there is no whip), and not through subjugation to some alpha animal (there is no alpha sled dog), but from the sheer joy of running in unison.

The food doled out by the driver forms a bond between him and the dogs but could not induce an animal unfitted for the task to run all day. They run from joy.

This thesis, the Coppingers note, might seem far-fetched. But they ask the reader to consider human courtship rituals. We humans enjoy these rituals for and in themselves; we are genetically wired to do so. We do not delight in them for their ability to achieve for us a mate—such end is an ancillary (and—if I may—to men, a surprising) end to the process.

Sexual intercourse, similarly, is enjoyable in itself, irrespective of and unrelated to its biologically engineered purpose: the creation of offspring.

We human beings delight in drama. We will vote, against our own best interests, for the side presenting its case most dramatically. We will endorse war, we will *fight* in wars whose benefit, in hindsight, consisted solely in the dramatic confection of national unity.

Oscar Hammerstein II most correctly summed it up: "Fish gotta swim, birds gotta fly." And we humans need to indulge in drama. What, then, when we do not?

The terrier, as per the Coppingers, needs to hunt small rodents. This is its joy. It loves to ferret out, to dig, to nip. It continues to practice its joyful innate behaviors, even in the absence of rodents. Their practice, now, however, has a new name: it is called "behavioral difficulties."

And our need to explain the world, to understand cause and effect, that joyful, innate capacity that we call "intelligence" and that we say separates us from the animals, that capacity *will* be exercised. We may employ it at the theater, which is only an experience of the story around the campfire; in gossip, and that formalized gossip we call "journalism"; in that particular subset of gossip known as politics; and in neurotic behavior in the home, the workplace, and the community.

Each of the above is the retelling or the *acting out* (the enjoyable discharge) of a dramatic, cohesive, incited, and completed view of the world.

These are the neurologic or, if I may, the phylogenetic underpinnings of drama.

Or, perhaps, the enthused individual might be charmed by the psychoanalytic paradigm. This person might see, in the formation of neurosis or psychosis, the dramatic tendency *en petit*.

For dreams and drama are the same. The power of dreams to affright, instruct, amuse, and trouble the individual might be analyzed and the fruit of that investigation applied to the construction of the drama.

Psychoanalysis is an attempt to discern in ostensibly unconnected actions and images a simple, hidden, unifying theme and, as such, may be seen as the absolute and perfect inversion of the dramatist's work.

The dramatist begins with a theme, or *quest,* and endeavors to describe its progression in ostensibly unconnected actions and images that will, at the quest's conclusion, be revealed as unified, and that revealed unity will simply state the theme, which revelation will—just as, theoretically, with the revelation by the analysis—restore order.

The rules of drama are few, its practice difficult, its implications many and fascinating.

But apart from a presentation of these few rules, the work of half a morning, what might be the purpose or, indeed, the content of a graduate course in screenwriting?

Perhaps this graduate course is designed to prepare one for the rigors, not of creation itself but of presentation, comportment, packaging—in fine, the glad-hand, one-must-take-one's-pigs-to-market aspect of any creative art, or indeed, of any business.

Such a course of study would, of necessity, involve chicanery, euphemism, obfuscation, suppression, repacking, or rechanneling of the natural instincts of aggression, ambition, greed, and envy—the skills of business, in effect.

For one must take one's pigs to market, and any market is run by the middlemen.

These middlemen in Hollywood are bureaucrats, and they have a natural foe, and this foe is the script. For a star's grosses may be quantified, and a prediction (supportable even when proved false) may be made about his or her worth. But the worth of a script is moot.

How, then, to remove the potential (not for *error* but for *recrimination*) of an unfortunate choice?

By removing the unquantifiable: the surprising, the unique, the upsetting, the off-color, the provocative; by removing *drama*. A course in the *business* of screenwriting, then, might teach how to recognize, in order to obliterate, drama.

Skill in this bureaucratic endeavor, unfortunately, will avail the practitioner little, as in shunning the original, he consigns himself to a limitless applicant pool—to a pool made up of all those capable of suppressing, or incapable of possessing, a love of drama. But, again, one would not have to sign up for X years of graduate schooling in order to learn this skill.

Of what use is this graduate film diploma, then? As evidence of the bona fides of the applicant. For someone capable of putting up with X years of the nonsense of school would be odds-on willing to submit to the sit-down-and-shut-up rigors of the bureaucratic environment.

Perhaps, then, this graduate course functions, whether through design or happy accident, not to *train* but to certify house slaves.

Or perhaps this graduate course is the modern equivalent of what we ancients know as music appreciation class, wherein the students were awarded credit for listening to select tunes and praised for repeating back the phrases they had been instructed to associate with them.

Perhaps this graduate course is a congruent Pavlovian endeavor. But I suspect it is the boot camp of that side world, "the industry."

For the privileged class, in this or any other society, must take care of its own. So just as children of privilege may not "take" but may only "experiment with" drugs, the privileged may not be "out of work" but, to the contrary, be "searching for themselves." And lest this search prove too rigorous, they might relax for several years in film school watching movies.

After which point, those sufficiently connected may wave their diplomas and proceed into the studio system.

Meanwhile, back at the ranch, let us leave our suppository graduate school and investigate actual hard-won, practicable, real-world dramatic skills.

The entire practicable sentence was, of course, not "Cut to the chase" but "When in doubt, cut to the chase." Good thinking.

Other filmmakers' pearls—seldom wrong, always instructive—follow:

"Stay with the money." The audience came to see the star. The star is the hero; the drama consists solely in the quest of the hero.

"You start with a scalpel and you end with a chainsaw." Don't be too nice about cutting the film; throw away everything that's not the story.

"In the morning you're making *Citizen Kane;* after lunch you're making *The Dukes of Hazzard.*" At some point you're going to start running out of time. Plan your time by sticking to the essential story. You're going to cut everything else anyway.

These gems and their like can be learned only on the set, or in the editing room, while actually making a film.

But, the chauvinists sigh, concealing their exasperation with my Jacobin views, you forget that one *may,* at this graduate school, *actually make films.*

Yes and no.

For the real skills of filmmaking can actually be learned and practiced only in relation to an audience.

If the audience is financially involved (the studio executives), suborned (the "invited" carded test-group screening), or hired (the university professors), one will learn nothing from their responses except obedience.

The actual dramatic audience has suspended its disbelief and has sat down in order to be thrilled (in contradiction to the groups named above, that come, each in its own way, to pursue its particular goal).

Very well, but, the chauvinists continue, may not these

actual academic student filmmakers *take* their film, escaping from the academy with this golden goose, and show it to a wider world?

Sure thing; but, then, what did the school contribute?

But what of the scholarship student, what of he who could not afford tuition and entered the school only as a way to achieve, without cost, the film cameras and lights unattainable in the lay world?

The school, then, exists as a primarily charitable institution?

Fine, and all power to the young filmmaker who managed to take advantage of it. *This* person, however, would proceed directly to defrauding the chumps who thought they were doing him a good turn and divert their right-thinking charity to his own necessary ends—just as he will have to when he has moved to the wider world.

Bravo.

And as for the graduate school, so for the undergraduate and the various limitless seminars in filmmaking dotting our coasts and increasingly making inroads upon the hinterland.

They may be a rest stop for the insufficiently aggressive (those folks will find their rest expanded into a lifetime career), they may be a film club for those who cannot take their entertainment straight, they may be a boot camp for those desirous of becoming efficient at submission, or they may be a pen to hold and fleece the children of the privileged. But I think perhaps they have little to do with the actual making of movies.

THE SCRIPT

It all comes down to the script, or as they say in the theater, "If it ain't on the page, it ain't on the stage."

A good script may shine with superb actors, and a great script can be done well with amateurs. (Note the times one has heard or said, "I saw a high school amateur community production of *Waiting for Godot, Our Town, The Winslow Boy,* et cetera, and, do you know, it was perhaps the best thing I've ever seen.")

Now, when you get a great script done with great actors, then you have a classic.

The Godfather, A Place in the Sun, Dodsworth, Galaxy Quest—these are perfect films. They start with a simple premise and proceed logically, and inevitably, toward a conclusion both surprising and inevitable. The godfather wants to protect his best-loved son from contamination by the family criminal enterprise; the son eventually becomes the godfather. An attractive, poor, and ambitious young man worships wealth and beauty; he is eventually offered both beyond his wildest dreams, but his lust, as he sought them, leads him to kill the woman who would mar his plans, and he ends, on the brink of "success," caught and executed for his crime. A washed-up bunch of television actors curse the long-gone success of their show; it has mired them in supermarket openings, portraying cutout heroes; they are given the chance to inhabit that fantasy-turned-real and discover, in themselves, real heroism.

The stories are easy to summarize, as they are easy to follow. Every event in these stories can be plotted as a point on the progression described.

That is one definition of a great screenplay.

That which enthuses the actors and director enthuses the audience. To wit, I have been told the operative premise, and I want to know what happens next.

The film's precursor is the story around the campfire. In that story we hear and we imagine; in the film we see and we imagine. The structural nature of film allows the imagination to reign.

When the film turns narrative rather than dramatic, when it stands in for the viewer's imagination, the viewer's interest is lost.

The dramatic structure relies exclusively upon the progression of incident. How do we identify an *incident*? An incident (as per Aristotle) is a necessary step from the beginning proposition (a mafia don wants to spare his son the life of a criminal) to the conclusion (the son becomes the criminal chief).

To recur to the campfire story analogy, "But then the ship struck the rock and began to sink in the cold and angry sea," is better than "But then the ship struck a large, gray, wet, and ragged rock and began to sink into a frothing, viciously cold, tumultuous sea, its riptides roaring, its calmer regions full of man-eating sharks."

The rule, then, in filmmaking, as in storytelling, as in writing, is "leave out the adjectives."

Enter: *Rock Lindquist*. He's a funny kind of guy. He walks with a swagger, but perhaps it masks an inner insecurity. Women find this attractive. They want to mother him. *We* do, too. . . .

This trash is, unfortunately, the stuff that makes, to a script reader, a "good read."

It distracts the reader, the writer, the producer, and the actor from the only question *(what is, in fact, happening?)* that would allow them to make a rational, let alone an artistic, choice. It is the coin of the realm.

The film may, perhaps, be likened to a boxer. He is going to have to deal with all the bulk his opponent brings into the ring. Common sense should indicate he had better not bring one extra ounce of flab on him—that all the weight *he* brings into the ring had better be muscle.

The extra scene: no film can stand it.

When, again, is a scene superfluous? When it does not advance the progression given at the outset as the film's purpose. What happens during this side trip? The audience's attention wanders. They have been jolted out of participation, and the filmmaker has lost his most important ally: their uncritical, which is to say, engaged, participation.

How may one learn the absolute primacy of the script?

Shoot for show, cut for dough—Hollywood has it that one learns to shoot in the editing room. It is there that the honeymoon ceases and the marriage begins. The filmmaker, wedded to the footage he has shot, now, over the breakfast table, if you will, must evaluate his choice and figure out how to live with it.

"How could I have been so foolish" invariably refers to the script and its lack of precision; and the filmmaker may well refer, to extend the connubial analogy, to the wisdom of Berry Gordy and Smokey Robinson, in their 1960 hit "Shop Around": "Pretty girls come a dime a dozen, try to find one who's gonna give ya true lovin'."

Helpful hints to the filmmaker and the viewer: The compliments—"What visuals!" "What craft!" "What use of the camera!" and "What technique!"—all mean "the script stinks."

WOMEN, WRITING FOR

What about writing for women? Some men can, and some men can't.*

I recommend John le Carré's Connie Sachs, the retired wizard of the British Secret Service, the truest and best ally of George Smiley. *There* is a portrait for you, and you can keep Blanche DuBois.

Read John Horne Burns's *The Gallery* for his whores of World War II Naples and, most particularly, for the good girl, Guilia. The ugly American captain falls in love, and his love is reciprocated. The good girl will marry him, wait for him, do anything, in short, except have sex with him before marriage. The major is about to return to combat; he calls her a demon. She looks at him surprised. "But," she says, "*all* women are."

Read John O'Hara if you'd like portraits of women by a man.

What do these depictions have in common? They are unsentimental. An absence of sentimentality is a great thing in a writer and separates the merely good from those who actually have something to say.

For it needs no prophet to remind us of the day's received wisdom—advertising will do that job quite nicely. The true writer must write not the acceptable but the true.

* The same is true of women.

True depiction of women is, I think, rather different from political sanctimony—and the political emancipation of women has given rise to a spate of pablum.

Vide the spontaneously emerging form of the women's movie. Five old friends get together to rehash their lives. All well and good. This film, however, is a prerogative of an increasingly healthy polity, not its description.

The lower classes of late seem to delight in depictions of women as victims of sex (abuse, rape, harassment); the more elevated, as victims of marriage.*

These efforts—whether of women or men—award a cheap obeisance; they are Mariolatry in its ultimate debasement: "Women are good, women are pure, how good are we to acknowledge their suffering."

As such they are also a form of emotional pornography, for, like *The Passion of the Christ* or *The Green Mile,* they may license the viewer to enjoy a disturbing spectacle through permitting him or her to protest revulsion at it.

But true depiction of women takes into account two things: the ways in which women are similar to men and the ways in which they are different.

For to say that all people are equal is not to say they are the same, and to confound the political with the practical gave us the enormity both of school busing and of feminist literary theory.

Actresses in Hollywood complain that there are no parts for women. There *are* parts for women, but they are few and

---

* The first category is sufficiently widespread to have, in Hollywood, its own cognomen, fem jep (females in jeopardy), e.g., all the Halloween, Friday the 13th films, *Blair Witch, Panic Room, Flightplan,* et cetera. The second category, grown out of the mid-Victorian sensation novel, survives as *The Ice Storm, The Joy Luck Club, Thelma & Louise,* et cetera. Essentially a form of whining, this "marriage as feminine ordeal" category seems to be waning in popularity as a younger audience of women increasingly accepts many of the gains of the feminist movement as a matter of course.

tend to go to the nubile. This may be good or bad, but it is true.

Is it the job of the movies to offer a well-balanced distribution-by-gender of roles? If so, who would make the choice?

Who but the slighted, seeking, as most of us do when accepting that role, not universal justice, but reparations? Even the dramatic roles for women, when viewed not as entertainment but as, if I may, art, are drivel—*Now, Voyager; Sophie's Choice;* and *Flightplan*—treating us to the noble spectacle of women either crying or bravely not crying.

Is this "writing for women"?

Well, it is writing *about* women. Or about their simulacrum. Tennessee Williams, Truman Capote, Noël Coward wrote women characters that were fantasies of men by homosexual men. Enjoyable, indeed. But hardly accurate.

What is the truth about women?

Jacqueline Kennedy was seen, in the Zapruder film, crawling out of the back of the limousine in which her husband had just been shot. The wise and kind suggested she was going for help. Lenny Bruce accurately observed that she was "hauling ass to save her own ass," and was hounded out of show business.

But would not you, and would not I, do the same (which was his message) to escape from that fusillade? What was the hypocrisy intended to protect?

The "enlightened" Western view of women—that is, the currently politically acceptable depiction of women in art, is neurotic: Diana may be a princess or she may be a whore, but that's it. Women, in mass entertainment, may be victims or postsexual comrades—eunuchs, in effect: kind old men sitting on the porch wondering where they went wrong and emerging, somehow, better for the experience.

What about the real women, and may depictions of them be written by men?

Well, who is to say? The terrible voices of that coercion known as political correctness cry—but they cry not for parity, let alone for humanity, but for power.

Let us apply, to authors, a rational application of the rational doctrine of sexual equality: Is it less heinous to inquire the sex of an applicant for our attention than of an applicant for employment? Having settled that, let us move on—and hush up, you academics, brownnosing for tenure with your authors listed by sex, race, and geographical distribution. (Who asked you?)

The sex of the author is nobody's business—which can, politics aside, be established in fact by this simple test: How many choose films based on the sex of the creator? All right, then, let us apply the same standards to literature (where questions of taste may, *disons le mot,* be corrupted by an educationally induced hypocrisy) that we do to entertainment. In entertainment, we make our true, unfettered choices based on content and worth, not on politics.

I am reminded of the memoirs of an old sixties radical. He wrote that he had been gently pursued by a gay chum for forty years and, being straight himself, had politely declined. One day, however, it occurred to him that perhaps he was being politically incorrect, and so he went to bed with the guy. Fun's fun, but that, to me, is going too far.

The question is not can one sex write for the other—if not, are we then to have only unisexual dramas?—but can the individual *write*? That is, can he (a) see and (b) tell the truth?

Lenny Bruce's remark was unacceptable because it was true.

My play *Oleanna,* when it opened in 1992, was a *succès de scandale,* a handy French phrase meaning that everyone was so enraged by it that they all had to see it.

What about this play, a rather straightforward classical tragedy, drove people berserk?

It asserted that a person could make an accusation, the truth or supportability of which was open to debate.

One would not think this enraging, *but* the accusation was made by a young female student against a male professor, and the accusation was of rape.

The play's first audience was a group of undergraduates from Brown. They came to a dress rehearsal. The play ended and I asked the folks what they thought. "Don't you think it's politically questionable," one said, "to have the girl make a false accusation of rape?"

I, in my ignorance, was stunned. I didn't realize that it was my job to be politically acceptable. I'd always thought society employed me to be dramatic; further, I wondered what force had so perverted the young that they would think that increasing political enfranchisement of a group rendered a member of that group incapable of error—in effect, rendered her other than human.

For if the subject of art is not our maculate, fragile, and often pathetic humanity, what is the point of the exercise?

HOW SCRIPTS GOT SO BAD

Here's how they got so bad.

The entry-level position at motion picture studios is *script reader*. Young folks fresh from the rigors of the academy are permitted to beg for a job summarizing screenplays. These summaries will be employed by their betters in deliberations.

These higher-ups rarely (some, indeed, breathe the word "never") read the actual screenplay; thus, the summaries, called "coverage," become the coin of the realm.

Now, like anyone newly enrolled in a totalitarian regime, these neophytes get the two options pretty quickly—conform or die. Conformity, in this case, involves figuring out *what* the studios might like (money) and giving them the illusion that the dedicated employee, through strict adherence to the mechanical weeding process, can provide it. The script reader adopts the notion that inspiration, idiosyncrasy, and depth are all very well in their place but that their place has yet to be discovered and that he would rather die than deviate from received wisdom.

The mere act of envisioning "the public," that is, "that undifferentiated mass dumber than I," consigns the script reader to life on the industrial model. He or she now is no longer an individual but a field boss, a servant of "industry," and, as the industry in question deals with the mercantilization of myth, an adjunct of oppression. Deprived of the joys of whimsy, contemplation, and creation, they are left with prerogative. So script coverage is brutal and dismissive.*

Why would this canny employee vote for the extraordinary? The industrial model demands conformity, and the job of the script reader is not to discover the financially, and perhaps morally, questionable "new" but to excel in what, for want of a better word, one must call hypocrisy.

Oh, boo hoo.

Opposed we find the scriptwriter.

As the grosses of blockbuster movies swell, the quality falls. The viewers see this trash and, correctly, exclaim, "Well, *hell, I could do that!*" They then write a screenplay. These screenplays are, in effect, tickets to the lottery.

The late IPO delusion, the "new economy," has taken its place with the South Sea Bubble and the Dutch Tulip Mania. These short-lived and second-class frenzies are as nothing compared to the long-lived, indeed, unkillable fantasy that

---

* Though the script reader, producer, studionik may *subjectively* (and legitimately) dislike any given script on its merits, he is also not only liable but likely to dislike it because of the purely mechanical operation of the development process. The monied progenitor endorses the creation of a script based on a rose-colored prospectus, known as a "pitch." However good the commissioned script may actually *be,* it is certain to awaken in the sugar daddy or mommy a feeling of disappointment because of his or her outrage that it is not "the pitch." In this fit of pique, the executive, however, is operating under a delusion similar to that undergone by the radio listener meeting in the flesh the possessor of a beloved voice. The listener inevitably thinks, "*That's* not how I envisioned him *at all!*" not recognizing that he, the listener, never *did* envision the radio personality. He just listened to his voice, the sound of which created in the listener a feeling of familiarity *similar to* that created by cognizance of an individual's physical appearance. So the surprised radio listener thinks, "That's not how I envisioned him," rather than, "Oh. *That's* what he looks like"; and the producer thinks of the script, "That's not what I had in mind," *as if* (as is not the case) he actually had a concrete prevision of an actual forthcoming script. Which he did not. He had only a warm gooshy feeling engendered by the pitch.

each and every person born can rise to prominence and wealth in show business.

This sweet folly is a capitalist's erotic dream. In general, the theoretical limit to which wages can be reduced is that at which starvation transforms worker competition into revolution. (In plain English, the boss usually has to pay the workers *something*.) In show business, however, the bitten will not only work for nothing, they will also fight for the chance to do so.

Back at the ranch, the corrupted youth, the script readers, sit at what I will imagine as their high Victorian desks and paw through the incoming screenplays, nuzzling the earth for truffles for their masters. Yes, their muzzles are tied, but someday, someday *they*, these readers, may be elevated to the rank of executive—indeed, perhaps to the very pinnacle of studio head, where they will have the power not only to *discard* but actually to endorse. They will there be showered with perquisites, first and not least among them, that they will never again have to read another screenplay.

What, however, of the *professional* screenwriter? This person, cursed with actual dramatic sense and credentials, is, similarly, self-caught in an evil net. He differs from the amateur in that he is actually getting paid for the work. This puts hummus on the table but places him at a distinct disadvantage in the lottery of production.

There are two counts against him. First, the work—if it contains inspiration, glee, sorrow; if it is complex, actually provocative or disturbing—may not be easily condensable to those three sentences allowed the script reader. Second, the fact of his *actually getting paid* enrages those involved in the studio system. Is it not monstrous, they wonder, that one should actually *pay* for that which 90 percent of all human life would do for free? The two burdens of the actual writer, his inspiration and his bill, conjoin synergistically to end in tragedy.

Most writing assignments begin with the plea "Fireman, fireman save my child" and end "Where is that half-eaten chicken I believe I left in the icebox yesterday?"

For, in fine, most executives consider the writer a thief.

BEGGING LETTERS

The language of the modern screenplay is like that of the personals column. The descriptions of the protagonist and the lovelorn aspirant are one: beautiful, smart, funny, likes long walks and dogs, affectionate kind, honest, sexy. These descriptions, increasingly, are the content of the screenplay—replacing dialogue and camera angles, the only two aspects of a screenplay actually of use.

These new screenplays are essentially begging letters, that is: See how I paint myself in the best and most general of terms and beg that someone will recognize my abasement and meet my very human but, unfortunately, mutually exclusive needs. I beg, in effect, to be both recognized for my worthlessness and to be given love.

Note that a more potentially successful strategy in a personal ad might include a personal code: an obscure reference to the literary if one wants to entrap a reader, to the stock market to attract a financier, perhaps to the Bible to collar a person of religious beliefs.

Such are not found in the personals, as, I believe, the writers might think (correctly) that to specify actual desires or attributes might limit the applicant pool of potential respondents.

The correct place to find a perfect physique is in the gym, a religious person in shul or church, a book lover at the library.

But the writer of the personal ads appeals, in extremity, to the populace at large, throwing him- or herself on its mercy and begging for a date, with this unstated reservation: "I will figure it out later—just get me on the playing field." This appeal is addressed to the similarly hopeful and desperate: "Let us indulge in codependent behavior—we will, at the very least, have *that* to share. We each know the other is far from perfect, sexy, fun, brilliant, talented, soulful, and kind, and we will agree that this frank collusion is the magical incantation necessary to establish goodwill."

The problem lies in this: these ads establish little else, and any actual date must not end, but in fact *begin,* with a measure of disappointment.

So with the screenplay.

Here, in the character description, we are told that the heroine is various things that one might find attractive in a heroine, but should the writer's words be put upon the screen, they will be found wanting, for the hopeful description of the character will not have, magically, transformed itself to the screen. We can write, "She's the kind of girl *who* . . ." all day long, but neither the actress nor the director can actually implement it; and we find, in what practice proves is nonspecific and nonimplementable language, nothing but the desire of the writer to please.

What is wrong with trying to please?

Nothing at all. *But* the writer of the "lazy Sunday mornings" gobbledegook has worked not to please the *audience* but the executive (his codependent, desired other).

Just as the personal ad is written not to attract anyone specifically but only to avoid exclusion, the "lazy Sunday mornings" screenplay strives to appeal to all—or to those who think it might appeal to all. In this it also resembles a political speech, written to lull and, by its soporific cadence and vocabulary, to allow the listener to intuit whatever the hell she wants.

"Smash, bash, crash: the world became a steel cauldron of pain." "Yes," says the young script reader. "Yes. Hot stuff *indeed*. Boss? This is hot stuff. *This* person knows how to write action."

"Loves hazy afternoons. This well-educated beauty finds loveliness all around her. Perhaps *you* do, *too* . . . ?"

(SECRET BONUS CHAPTER)
THE THREE MAGIC QUESTIONS

Here is the long-lost secret of the Incas. Anyone who wants to know how to write drama must learn to apply these questions to *all* difficulties. It is not only unnecessary but also impossible to know the answers before setting out on the individual project in question, as there are no stock answers.

This secret of the Incas, then, is like the Torah, beloved of my people, the Jews. We read the Torah, the five books of Moses, every year, in the same order. Every year the meaning of the Torah changes, though the text remains unchanged.

As the writer changes, year to year, his or her perceptions and interests change. At twenty he is interested only in sex, at thirty in sex and money, at forty in money and sex, at sixty in money and validation, et cetera.

No one can write drama without being *immersed in* the drama. Here's what that means: the writer will and must go through *exactly* the same process as the antagonist (for what is the antagonist but a creation of the writer?).

The writer may choose to supply stock, genre, or predictable answers to the magic questions, and the drama will be predictable and boring. The writer will have saved himself the agony of indecision, self-doubt—of work, in short—and so, of course, will the protagonist. The audience will view this pseudo-drama much as the graduate views a liberal arts education:

"I don't think anything happened, but I'm told I went to college, so, perhaps, I somehow got an education."

All right, you may complain, get to the fairy dust portion of the entertainment and vouchsafe to me the secret of the Incas.

Here it is.

The filmed drama (as any drama) is a succession of scenes. Each scene must end so that the hero is thwarted in pursuit of his goal—so that he, as discussed elsewhere, is forced to go on to the next scene to get what he wants.

If he is forced, the audience, watching his progress, wonders *with* him, how he will fare in the upcoming scene, as the film is *essentially* a progression of scenes. To write a successful scene, one must stringently apply and stringently answer the following three questions:

1. Who wants what from whom?
2. What happens if they don't get it?
3. Why now?

That's it. As a writer, your *yetzer ha'ra* (evil inclination) will do everything in its vast power to dissuade you from asking these questions of your work. You will tell yourself the questions are irrelevant as the scene is "interesting," "meaningful," "revelatory of character," "deeply felt," and so on; all of these are synonyms for "it stinks in ice."

You may be able to dissuade your *yetzer ha'ra* by insisting that you were and are a viewer before you were a writer, and that as a writer, these three questions are all you want to know of a scene. (You come late to a film and ask your friend there before you, "What's going on? Who is this guy? What does he want?" and your friend will, as a good dramaturge, explain that the subject of your inquiry [the hero] is the vice president of Bolivia, and he wants to determine where his boss is, as the bad guys are going to ambush him, and if he, our hero vice president, does not extract the info from the reluctant mistress, whom the president has just thrown over, the bad guys will kill his boss and bring down the country.)

1. Who wants what from whom?
2. What happens if they don't get it?
3. Why now?

As one becomes more adept in the use of these invaluable ancient tools, one may, in fact, extend their utility to the level of the actual spoken *line* and ask of the speech, no doubt beginning, "Jim, when I was young I had a puppy. . . ." "Wait a second, how does this speech help Hernando find out where his boss, the president of Bolivia, is?" And you may, then, be so happy—not with the process but with the *results* of your assiduous application of these magic questions—that finding the puppy speech wanting in their light, you will throw it to the floor and out of the scene it was just about to ruin.

These magic questions and their worth are not known to any script reader, executive, or producer. They are known and used by few writers. They are, however, part of the unconscious and perpetual understanding of that group who *will* be judging you and by whose say-so your work will stand or fall: the audience.

TECHNIQUE

STORYTELLING:
SOME TECHNICAL ADVICE

Storytelling is like sex. We all do it naturally. Some of us are better at it than others.

One learns through experience, but basically, it is a universal human instinct, and I will prove it to you.

Explaining your particular plight to the traffic cop is creating a drama. Talking your way out of a late date, a forgotten anniversary; talking a potential partner into bed, a boss into a raise, a supplier into a discount—each of these is a drama.

The bedtime stories we have heard or told are dramas, and each partakes of the same natural form as the improvisations listed above: once upon a time, and then one day, and just when everything was going so well, and just at the last moment, and they all lived happily ever after. This is the form we learn at Mother's knee, and it is the form we apply in order to understand life. It casts us, the listener, as hero of our own personal drama, as, of course, we are, and it explains that drama to us in the way nature has fitted us to understand it: as a simple, honest attempt to achieve a worthwhile goal.

On our way to the goal (the wedding party, the discount, the weekend in Vegas), we encounter resistance, we find unforeseen reserves of strength and cunning, we are almost undone by some evil force (nature, fate, the traffic cop), and we eventually triumph by recourse to those basic precepts or powers that we were apprised of at the story's opening.

Our simplicity allows us to inform the king that he has no clothes; our inventiveness, to charm the cop; our work ethic, to deliver a superior product at an economical price and so become rich.

And that's it. That is all drama comes down to.

Now, why are some folks challenged in creating it?

There are two answers: (1) everybody can throw a ball, but not everyone can throw like Sandy Koufax; and (2) self-consciousness doth make dullards of us all.

Consider the making of a speech.

We are all, again, fairly accomplished speakers given the right setting. The speech to the wayward son comes flowing to the lips, liquid, satisfying, and pleasant. It comes extempore, it needs no preparation, and though we may be saddened by its lack of result, we are never other than enamored of its sound.

Take the same speaker, however, and tell him he is about to address the Rotary on the subject of the wayward son, and you are likely to find an endless heavy hell of bombast and cliché. What happened?

He forgot that he knew how to do it naturally.

Candidates for office in our fair land sound, for all the world, each like his dull brother or sister. Their wise wranglers have instructed them to "sound presidential" or "senatorial" or what have you, and, indeed, they do, if the holder of that office must sound like a boring dolt.

We are told of each of these bores that he or she is a load of laughs off camera, and who am I to disbelieve? But *on* camera they are a fate worse than death.

They have convinced themselves, or engaged others to convince them, to forget what they know.

None of these speakers would vote for himself if all he knew of himself was the stolid, lethal stump speech.

And yet, here is a fellow or a lass who, to reach the elevated position of his or her candidacy, has had to convince a vast number of rational people of the improbable; he talked fast and fascinatingly in the quest for the candidacy. The candidate forgot that he knows how to tell a story. As does the neophyte dramatist.

How does it go?

Once upon a time, and then one day, and just when everything was going so well, when just at the last minute, and they all lived happily ever after. Period.

Knute Rockne All American, The Greatest Story Ever Told, Hamlet, Dumbo, The Godfather all utilize the same form. (In the case of certain drama and tragedy, the happily ever after is, of course, altered, per case, to, for example, "And then they all lived sadder but wiser" [the drama] or "And then, finally realizing the essence of the human condition, they put their eyes out and wandered around for a while as a blind beggar" [tragedy].)

ONCE UPON A TIME

There was a poor but honest woman, who lived with her son, Jack, in the forest.

AND THEN ONE DAY

Their money ran out, and they were forced to sell their cow.

Jack was sent to take the cow to the fair.

On the way he met a man who offered Jack this bargain: I will trade you your cow for these five magic beans. The little boy happily made the change and came back to tell his mother the happy news.

AND JUST WHEN EVERYTHING WAS GOING SO WELL

She cursed him out for a fool, threw the beans out of the window, and retired to her bed, weeping.

The little boy went to sleep, and as he slept, the beans took root and grew, until the beanstalk reached clear to the sky.

On awakening, he climbed the beanstalk and discovered, in the clouds, a giant's castle. He entered the castle and saw inside of it treasures beyond imagining. There was a golden harp and a goose that laid golden eggs.

Thinking to redeem himself, he picked up the goose and made for the beanstalk. The goose began squawking and awoke the giant, who pursued Jack.

The giant grew closer and closer as Jack threw himself onto the beanstalk and started to descend.

The giant came on roaring, and Jack's end was at hand.

WHEN JUST AT THE LAST MINUTE

Jack reached the bottom, grabbed an axe, and cut down the beanstalk; and the giant fell to his death.

AND THEY ALL LIVED HAPPILY EVER AFTER.

We may apply the same paradigm to any drama. In some, one section will predominate over another—that is, some sections, case by case, will be lengthy and elaborate, some will be relatively short or simply indicated, but all will be present in each.

Every man of my age learned how to sharpen a knife. We learned it in the Boy Scouts.

One holds the knife at a 20-degree angle to the whetstone and cuts toward the oilstone. When a good enough bevel is obtained, the blade is turned, and the other side is sharpened.

But a friend of mine, Bill Bagwell, master knifesmith and a world-class expert, says that method is wrong.

Bill makes fighting and hunting knives by hand at an outdoor forge. His knives are prized by collectors and soldiers and hunters. He says one *drags* the blade over the stone rather than cutting into it. This turns the edge of the metal onto the far side of the blade. One then turns the blade and wipes this "wire edge" off.

This method works like mad. Bill used to demonstrate his wares at knife shows by cutting through several two-by-fours with his knife, cutting many inches of free hanging hemp rope, and then shaving the hair on his arm with the same blade. He'd then dull it so that one could safely draw one's thumb across it, give it a few strokes on the whetstone in his heretical fashion, and repeat the demonstration of fine and fancy cutting. QED.

I spent many years target shooting with pistols, and I became somewhat proficient through dedication to what I understood to be the two sole but inviolable rules for pistol accuracy: concentrate on the front sight and squeeze the trigger.

Again, any and all books on marksmanship contain the same advice. All wrong. The appurtenant Galileo in this case was Eric Haney, a friend who spent two decades in Delta Force as a professional gunfighter. To shoot competitively in the real world, learn to thrust the weapon toward the target, forget about the sights, and slap the trigger. That was the method he learned, taught, and trusted his life to over countless trials, and, obviously, it worked, as he had lived to correct me.

Bishop Berkeley wrote that the test of truth is "Would you trust your life to it?"

The film business has been, for a hundred years, the baili-wick of the empiricist: Ashkenazi peddlers, my cultural and racial brothers, battled to put food on the table by exhibiting moving pictures to a paying public. As the business grew, the canny hucksters, now one, now another, got a "good idea" about how to put more asses in the seats.

As the business attracted—then as now—the ne'er-do-well, these ideas were generally efficient. (As the ancient law has it, if you want to get a difficult job done, give it to a lazy man.)

Like new parents, the first movie folk had responsibility but no instruction book. And so they made it up as they went along:

The scene is supposed to be shot in the tropics, but it's cold on the beach in Santa Monica, and the actors' breath is frost-ing. Have them suck on ice before the take. The star can't cry? Put glycerin on her cheeks. *High Noon* is a dud? Insert shots of a ticking clock and cut to it as often as possible.

Look at the shot in *The Godfather, Part II,* where Rob-ert De Niro shoots the vicious mafioso don somebody-or-other. De Niro puts a gun to his head, pulls the trigger, and a vast wound opens in the don's forehead.

I asked how it was accomplished—did the gun spray the wound on? How could that be, as the wound appeared to have great depth? Here's how they did it. The makeup man built the wound into the actor's forehead, covered it with a layer of flesh, and ran an ultrathin monofilament from the flesh covering to the muzzle of De Niro's pistol. When De Niro shot, he jerked his hand back, mimicking recoil; the line tore the covering free; and the wound appeared.

There are many scenes in *A League of Their Own* where the actresses, portraying a baseball team, heave the ball with fantastic speed and accuracy.

I asked the director how the actresses gained such skill. She said she simply filmed the sequences without the ball.

That is the fascination of actual moviemaking: How do you *do* it? And one is learning, and humbled, constantly.

I spent a sleepless night thinking about the cat in *The Diary of Anne Frank.*

In one of the best suspense sequences in the movies, Joseph Schildkraut comes downstairs from the attic where the Franks hide. There is a burglar in the house, and Schildkraut has to dispatch him. The burglar goes away, but before Schildkraut can close the door, a night watchman notices it ajar and calls over a couple of patrolling Nazis.

Schildkraut retreats to the attic, and all wait breathlessly while the Nazis scout the house below. Now comes the cat. She pads along a kitchen ledge in the hidden attic, she puts her head into a funnel resting on the ledge, she pushes the funnel toward the edge. Now everyone in the world holds his or her breath. Now the funnel goes *over* the ledge. But wait—the cat's head is stuck in the funnel.

Should the funnel drop off, the Nazis will hear and discover the hidden attic and kill all the inhabitants. But continue to wait—the cat now pulls its head, the funnel still on it, back *onto* the ledge, and now draws its head off. What a great sequence. But how did they do it?

I surmise that they stuck some tuna fish inside the funnel, surrounded it with glue, and turned the camera on. That would get the cat's head into the funnel, and stuck there, but then how did they get it over the ledge?

Perhaps, I reason, monofilament line. One prop guy easing the funnel over the edge, another heaving gently on another line to get it back.

Good idea. But now what do you do on take two?

The cat ain't going to put her head back into another gluey funnel. My knowledge of actual filmmaking is sufficient to consider that they just left the cat *glued to* the funnel and called it a day. This would involve shooting the cat shot *last* in the film, but why not? (Supervision of the rights of animals—and children, for that matter—on movie sets is largely hypothetical.)

But no, but no: the cat actually got her head *out* of the funnel at the end of the shot. All right, what about *magnets*?

1. Cat, with magnet hidden (or, indeed, *implanted*) in its neck, is lured to stick its head into a funnel smeared with tuna fish.
2. Funnel contains radio-controlled electromagnet. (I'm assuming such things exist.)
3. Two prop guys hold monofilament lines, one to ootz cat and funnel over the ledge, second to ootz it back.
4. Electromagnet is turned off, and grateful cat removes head from funnel.

In this scenario, I would shoot the cat sequence *first,* that is, before "establishing" the cat.

Vide: Set up four or five ledges, four or five different cats. Whichever cat-and-team first got the shot in the can, *that* cat would be the hero cat and play in the rest of the film.

This version, of course, would require many *many* cats standing by. At least a pair for each ledge.

Why? What happens if you get your shot, you establish your hero cat, and she gets run over by a milk truck or something? You're up the creek is what.

Back to the attic in Amsterdam.

There are only two things wrong with my proposed electro-magnetical solution:

1. It is too elaborate.
2. The gag is so *good,* it feels like something dreamed up on the set.

That is, here we are, filming the "Nazis almost find us" sequence, and someone, the director or AD, starts jumping up shouting "ooh ooh ooh"* and comes up with the cat. And the funnel.

Maybe not, but in my experience, the prop people and the stunt people are smarter about the gags (certainly than the writer, and regularly) than the director.

But in *this* case, the director was George Stevens. Now, George Stevens started out as assistant cameraman for Hal Roach, shooting Laurel and Hardy silents.

These, to me, are the perfection of essential moviemaking. Perfect simple plot, no distracting jabber (or "dialogue," as it is more generally known), and the only thing moving the film along is *gags*—that's all there is.

The gags, here, happen to be identical to Aristotle's "incidents," that is, *those occurrences without which the plot cannot move forward.*

Here, Mr. Stevens's great gag illustrates the conjunction of

* Those three words are inevitably the herald of film genius.

the artistic, the technical, and the administrative, which constitute the nature of the director's job.

1. Ooh ooh ooh, the cat puts his head in a funnel.
2. How do we make it work?
3. How do we arrange the schedule to make it possible, and how do we protect ourselves in the event of error or catastrophe?

I will give the cat gag one more think and then surrender.

The doctors say, "You hear hoofbeats, think horses, not zebras." So, to the filmmaker, Occam's razor is "they probably shot it backwards."

(E.g., *The Pride of the Yankees*. The story of Lou Gehrig, famous and famously left-handed hitter. Gary Cooper, playing the Iron Horse, bats righty, so they printed the Yankees logo backward and had Cooper bat right, hit, and then run to third.)

But, no, the cat can't be shot backward, because he both starts and *ends* with his head free of the funnel.

(If the cat started the shot with his head in the funnel and ended it free, one could simply film a cat free, who sticks his head in the funnel, and run the film backward.)

I start again, my reasoning:

1. There existed, in antiquity, a cat trained to stick her head in a funnel, inhale sufficiently to keep the funnel stuck onto the head, et cetera. . . .
2. I give up.

I will now proceed to that portion of the entertainment known as "duh."

I will telephone George Stevens Jr., and he will describe to me the simple, and now totally obvious, method his father used. I will slap my forehead and then share it with you.

While it remains a mystery, I will note some of my favorite effects.

In *Only Angels Have Wings*, Thomas Mitchell, ex-flyer and aircraft mechanic to flyer Cary Grant, stands on the field as Grant lands in his monoplane.

Mitchell takes a cigarette from his pack, places it in his mouth. We see Grant's plane on final, about to land. Mitchell takes a wooden match and holds it above his head. The plane— seen in the background—comes closer to touchdown. Now the plane is about to touch down, and the passage of its wing over Mitchell's upraised hand lights the match, and Mitchell lights his cigarette.

This is a conjunction of a *gag* (something done on the set) and an *effect* (something done in or using the talents of the lab). In this case, there is a rear-screen projection of the approaching plane, which dips just below frame at the last moment. A physical mock-up of the *wing* then replaces it and passes over Mitchell's head to light the match.

Another favorite: Note the shot of Munchausen's boat beaching on some island or other in Terry Gilliam's *The Adventures of Baron Munchausen*. We see the prow of the ship cutting through the water. Now the water lessens, and the boat continues cutting through the *sand*.

Note also: Julia Roberts getting into her car in *Erin Brockovich*. The car pulls out into traffic and then is demolished by an oncoming vehicle. (This is an *effect*: Julia actually swaps out her place with a stuntwoman early in the sequence, the two shots are melded in the lab, and the stuntwoman takes the hit.) Another magnificent effect is the running-upstairs shot in *Contact* (director Robert Zemekis, cinematographer Don Burgess), in which the camera pulls the hero, a little girl, down a corridor, up the steps, and toward a medicine cabinet holding the drugs that will save her father from his heart attack.

She reaches forward, and the shot of her face becomes a

shot of a medicine cabinet. The camera, however, does not move. That is, it is as if the entire shot were, somehow, a reflection in the medicine cabinet mirror. A stunning effect.

A brilliant gag is the murder of Alex Rocco in *The God-father*. His assassin (Franco Citti) kills Rocco (as Moe Greene) in the barber chair of the St. Regis.

Rocco is getting shaved. He senses something amiss and puts on his eyeglasses. The assassin fires, and Rocco's glasses shatter as he is shot in the eye.

How did they do that?

The eyeglass temples contained a miniscule BB apparatus and air gun. On cue, the BB was propelled forward, *from* the face, *toward* the lens.

I call George Stevens Jr., as I was saying, and plead for an answer. He laughs. This shot, it seems, is *already* a part of film lore.

Mr. Stevens tells me (to my pride) that (1) there *were* a bunch of cats, and (2) his father, the director, "just turned on the cameras and shot an *unbelievable* amount of film, waiting for *some* cat to do something 'uncatlike.'"

What a wonderful business.

The *gag*, again, is the script-in-miniature, one crystal clear idea, superseded by another, creating expectations dashed in a logical and surprising way, thus, of necessity, propelling us into the next beat.

This is the paradigm understood and practiced by commercial makers—a strict adherence to the rules of drama.

Hard enough to do in the one-gag format of the thirty-second commercial; *very* hard to do over the course of the ninety-minute film.

But the *mechanism* is identical and the key to great moviemaking.

It is an improvisation based on a conscious or intuited understanding of how an audience perceives:

a. Make them wonder.
b. Answer their question in a way both surprising and inevitable.

This is the exact same mechanism as the joke:

a. Do you wake up grumpy in the morning?
b. No, he gets up on his own.

Our delight in the joke—as in the drama—comes from our momentary triumph over that ever-vigilant repressive mechanism, that distinctive, questionable human gift that, otherwise, we are required to praise: our consciousness. Participation in the drama, as in the hunt, in sex, in war, and, curiously, at the movies, regresses us to an irreducible humanity.

IMPROVISATION

Near the end of filming a movie, I lose an important location, and several months of planning and preparation go out the window. This, however, must be viewed as a blessing, as it forces me to, once again, reduce the scene from the pictorial to the schematic.

What does this mean?

I had formulated my plan of filming in *shots*. One: shot of the wheels of the plane taxiing, hero appears behind them; two: shot of petrol dump with Arabic signs and English signs reading DANGER — INFLAMMABLE; three: Land Rover stopped by large construction barricade.

Now, with no more petrol dump and no more construction barricades, I must discard my pretty (if, as yet, only imagined) pictures and return to the theoretical. That is: *if* the hero wants to get the abducted girl home, and *if* the villain has discovered his plan and means to subvert it, what stratagems will each employ in the last reel?

I am forced back to the most simple: what does the Hero want, in this scene, and how can it be designed such that its exclusion or, indeed, replacement in the progression renders the story moot? One learns to ask, as something always will go wrong.*

* Perhaps I am being teased by providence. I wrote and directed a film called *State and Main* in which a movie company is kicked out of its small-town location

Steven Spielberg confessed, in a documentary on the making of *Jaws,* that the brilliance ascribed to him in withholding the appearance of the shark until halfway through that film must be credited, instead, to the mechanical shark, which refused to function when the cameras turned. The shark wouldn't swim, so the director had to come up with the standby plan. The revised plan showed not the shark but the *effects* of the shark or the location where one might *expect* the shark, and audiences screamed at the photograph of the water.

I once asked Bob Rafelson about what I found an interesting choice at the end of his *King of Marvin Gardens.* The girl comes into the room for a "talk" scene, hair dripping from a shower, wrapping her head in a towel.

"Oh yeah," he said, and explained: she had come to the set having unilaterally decided to chop off her long red, long-established hair. Rafelson had already shot both preceding and succeeding scenes, where she had hair down to her waist, so he threw her in the shower and told her come out and throw a towel around it.

I recall a close-up of Betty Hutton in *The Miracle of Morgan's Creek.*

Preston Sturges stages one of his beautiful walk-and-talks, pulling Betty and Eddie Bracken down the small-town street for three minutes of jabber. (Cf., by the way, Tim Holt in the pony cart in *The Magnificent Ambersons,* where Orson Welles dressed not one but *both* sides of the Main Street set—we see the shop fronts of one and, reflected in their windows, the traffic in the street and the shop fronts opposite.) Eddie Bracken and Betty walk down the street, and halfway through, their

---

two days before filming is to begin. Various gags in the first few minutes concern the absence in the new town of an old mill. The screenwriter shows up and is told, blithely, to deal with the problem and make the script conform to reality; we then discover that the film they are to shoot is *called The Old Mill.*

tracking two-shot becomes a grainy, blown-up close-up of Miss Hutton, when, as any filmmaker could explain, the lab or the director found an impossible error in the otherwise uncoveraged shot.

In English, Sturges had "shot the scene in one"—that is, his only coverage of the scene was the one shot, he had nothing he could cut *to,* and, so, when the developed film showed a scratch on the negative or a previously unsuspected light stand in the background, the director confected the close-up of Hutton by overenlarging her image from the two-shot.

I will further extend my foray into Sturgesiana by here revealing, for what *must* be the first time anywhere, and to what must be a severely restricted coterie of the interested in such minutiae, what must be Sturges's inspiration for a sequence in, and perhaps for his creation of, another of his films, *Hail the Conquering Hero*. Eddie Bracken is again Sturges's protagonist. His father was awarded the Medal of Honor in World War I, in the marines. Bracken enlists in the marines in World War II but is debarred from serving because of his hay fever. He is comforting himself in a bar when a group of combat marines, fresh from Guadalcanal, comes in. He buys them a drink and tells them his sad story—he has been writing home fictitious takes of his exploits in the corps and now cannot go home to face the lie.

The marines lend him a uniform and say they'll escort him back home, he'll get off the train, go home, kiss his mom, take off the uniform, and say he doesn't want to talk about the war. A perfect comic premise, a perfect comic film.*

---

* Let me add to my list of loves the opening shot of *Hail the Conquering Hero*. A sultry café singer croons "Safe in the Arms of Mother" to a bunch of drunks, but the camera does not dwell on her charms, no, but slips off to frame the enormous asses of two waiters who stroll the café with her, singing harmony— as if trying to find road room to overtake and again frame the hot tomato. This

Preston Sturges. Who turned William Demarest into a household god. To whom he gave the line, "This'll put Shakespeare back with the shipping news." Preston Sturges, who, in *The Lady Eve,* shepherded Henry Fonda through *five* pratfalls in half a minute, who—but I digress. So Mr. Bracken is escorted back to town by William Demarest and the Guadalcanal marines. His plan, to scoot from the railroad station the two blocks home, change into mufti, and that's the end of it. *But* word has gone afore, and the mayor has turned the town out. There are banners and competing brass bands. The whole town throngs the square. The train pulls up; one band plays "Hail the Conquering Hero" while the other plays "The Marine Corps Hymn," and Franklin Pangborn, avatar of the fey, tears out his remaining hair as the distraught master of ceremonies. What delight then, to discover the following:

Away the carriage goes! With the noisy populace about the wheels. What is this?—music? Yes: two opposition bands. One is playing "See the Conquering Hero Comes" while the other exhausts itself, and gets black in the face, with the exertion necessary in doing justice to "Rule Britannia."

—Mary Elizabeth Braddon,
The Trail of the Serpent (1885)

Over the years various journalists and other worthy folk have asked me, "Where do you get your ideas?" To which I usually reply, "I think of them." I permit myself this jolly facetiousness as the truth is, to me, more ghastly: (1) I have no idea; (2) I have so very few of them.

For film, in addition to being a structured dialectic (as per

Sergei Eisenstein), is a corporation of Good Ideas: Eisenstein's mutinous sailors herded beneath a tarpaulin to be shot in *Battleship Potemkin,* Spielberg's absence of a shark, William Wyler's tracking shot of Mary Astor and Walter Huston *just missing* each other in the American Express office in Naples (*Dodsworth,* my vote for one of the world's ten best films), George Stevens's shot of Elizabeth Taylor at the end of *A Place in the Sun.* She sits alone, and the fire in the fireplace is superimposed on her, reflected in the window.

Where *do* our ideas come from?

Perhaps the best, the true, are the reward neither of talent nor luck but of humility.

THE SLATE PIECE

Yet still the weak offender must beg still for leniency and trust his power to avoid the sin peculiar to his discipline.

—W. H. Auden

They say you get to make a movie three times: when you write it, when you shoot it, and when you cut it.

One really doesn't start to learn how to write a script until one has been on a set—on the set one learns the difference between what is *filmable* and what is merely pretty words. ("Outside the window, *New York*—in all its vicious splendor" is charming verbiage and all that, but, script-in-hand, on location, its director is going to be hard-pressed to learn from the script where to put the camera.)

Giving the actor a meaningful pause as part of his take may seem thoughtful and sensitive during filming, but the director stuck in the cutting room, watching the same interminable take, may learn, next time around, to *pick up the pace*.

The making of movies is magnificently pragmatic. As in combat, as in sex, the theoretical is all well and good if one's a commentator, but the thing itself can actually be understood only through experience. No one on any set, or in any cutting room, knows the difference (if such there is) between realism

and naturalism—they are merely "telling a story with pictures."
A couple of guys in a coffee shop set out to write a gag; a couple of guys with a camera set out to film a gag; a couple of guys in an editing room set out to make sense of the trash that's been dumped on their desks. That's moviemaking in its entirety—anything else is just "the suits." Through it all the clock is ticking: so many days and they take away the camera, so many days and the studio needs to release the print.

Stuck in a scene, in the editing room, sometimes the roof falls in: an actor has not picked up his cue, and the scene stops dead—there is no cutaway (no other actor to cut to, to "pace up" the sequence), and the movie grinds to a halt.

"If only," the director or editor says, "if *only* the actor sitting there like the sphinx had looked to his *left*: if he'd looked to his *left*, instead of his right, I could intercut his close-up with a shot of the other actor and pace up the scene."

But no, the actor never looked to his left, and the scene is doomed to death. But perhaps there is one hope.

The director says, "Check the slate piece."

What is the slate piece?

Here's how it goes: When the shot is set up, the actors are called in and placed. The sound guy calls "rolling," the camera is turned on, the operator tells the camera assistant to "mark it," the assistant puts the slate board (the once actual slate with chalk markings, now electronic) in front of the lens to record on film the shot's number and take. The shot is thus "slated," the director calls "action," and the take begins.

But, we may note, there was a moment, when the camera was filming, *before* the shot was slated, when the actor was waiting for action to be called. In this moment he *may* have looked to his left, his right, up or down, frowned, or smiled or yawned or done any number of things that just might magically come to the aid of a stalled or otherwise doomed shot.

This accidental, extra, hidden piece of information is called the slate piece. And most of moviemaking, as a writer, a director, a designer, is the attempt not to *invent* but to discover that hidden information—the slate piece—that is already lurking in the film.

THE WISDOM OF THE ANCIENTS

My friend Eric, career military, told me that he figured that the men who taught him in Vietnam had been taught by those who fought in World War II; that *they,* in turn, had been taught by the soldiers of World War I, who had been taught by the soldiers of the Spanish-American War, who had been taught by the Indian fighters; the hard-won direct hands-on knowledge being transmitted, by extension, to him from Thermopylae and Sumer.

Thermopylae and Sumer, in film, are, even now, just, *just* beyond living memory.

I got notes over the phone on my first screenplay from Samson Raphaelson, who wrote the first talkie.

I once had a drink with Dorothy Gish, who starred for D. W. Griffith; I made a film with Don Ameche, who was the world's biggest star in the early talkie era; I played poker for years with Eddie Bracken; the gaffer on the last film I shot is the grandson of the gaffer on *Intolerance*.

We find ourselves, still, that close to the beginning of the first new art since cave painting.

The earliest films were pure exploitation: a railroad train rushes at the viewer, a couple kisses. The novel technology put bread in the exhibitor's lunch pail.

Exhibitors found they could charge more for longer films, and greater length necessitated a dramatic structure. ("What gimmick," they wondered, "could we use to keep the audience docile between the thrills?") This same problem plagues the porn industry, which has addressed it by increasingly shortening the intervals between sex.

Mainline films have treated the problem similarly—periods between violence and sex diminish in an asymptote, the period gradually approaching the virtually nonexistent, such "spacer" material describable dramatically as "and *now*. . . ."

Multireel films created the necessity for scenarists, folks who could fill the gap between train wrecks. Their ranks included playwrights and novelists, who found themselves, from the first, in opposition to the money folk, the exhibitors, and the banks.

The exhibitors are, of course, in it for the money; films got longer in order to allow them to charge more; persons with a dramatic bent were brought on board to allow the films to grow longer, and found, and find, themselves squared off against exhibitors, who reason: "How is the audience going to be thrilled by a shot, a scene, a sequence, in which no one is being either kissed or killed?"

But dramatic structure consists of the creation and deferment of hope. That's basically all it is. The reversals, the surprises, and the ultimate conclusion of the hero's quest please in direct proportion to the plausibility of the opponent forces. The study of same, to the dramatist, scenarist, or, in the old days, "title writer," is the essence of film. These scribes brought and bring to the movies an ancient wisdom (or an approach to same), such wisdom stemming from a conscious or intuitive attempt to understand how human beings think.

What is the ancient wisdom?

Well. I suspect that a Spartan warrior, transplanted to a rifle platoon in Iraq, would find the situation rather familiar and would adapt to the new technology pretty quickly.

(The businesspeople who started the movies thought similarly: What difference selling moving pictures of a locomotive or selling gloves? It's just *selling*.)

And the dramatist, his calling older than that of the merchant and as old as the soldier's, similarly takes his skills, along with a racial intuition or predisposition, into the endeavor.

Here he is joined by the visual artist.

For the film, it has been discovered, cannot be merely the record of a stage play. It must tell the story, but it must tell it in *pictures*.

This is the new art, the conjunction of the dramatic and the plastic.

It has been approached in stagecraft and stage design, but the analogy is insufficient. Stage design exists to frame and intensify a drama of human scale; films can juxtapose seemingly random images to tell a dramatic story.

What prodigies of personal insight or of interpersonal collaboration and strife are necessitated by this new art, and how may one master its difficulties?

I've always been a delighted devotee of film wisdom, those distilled snippets of experience passed from the now-wiser to the newcomer—the wisdom of the ancients, some of which I now addend.

Stay with the money. The audience came because you advertised the star. Shoot the star. (NB: Howard Lindsay, coauthor of the plays *Arsenic and Old Lace, Life with Father, State of the Union,* et cetera, once privately printed a small volume of stage wisdom. One of his axioms was: take the great lines from the secondary characters and give them to the lead. This works like gangbusters in film and on stage. It raises the question: Why would the dramatist *want* to give the yummy lines to the second banana—as one *does;* the temptation to do so is great. Someone of a psychologic bent might suppose that the dramatist does so out of envy of the hero and the desire to show oneself superior. In any case . . .) Stay with the money.

Burn the first reel. Almost any film can be improved by throwing out the first ten minutes. That exposition, which assuaged the script reader, the coverage writer, the studio exec, the star and her handlers puts the audience to *sleep sleep sleep.* Get right into the action, and the audience will figure it out. (Simple test, for the unbelieving: when you walk into a bar and see a drama on the television, you've missed the exposition. Do you have any trouble whatever understanding what's going on?)

If you think that perhaps you should cut, cut. A film is made, and one learns to make film, first on the set but more importantly in the cutting room. If you suspect the shot, sequence, line is unnecessary, *get rid of it.* Like the dramatist giving the punch lines to the stooge, you, the filmmaker, can't quite trust yourself. Err on the side of the audience, and get on with it. Cf. "You start with a scalpel and end with an axe."

If you laughed at the dailies, you aren't going to laugh at the picture. Too true. Equally true of tears. That scene that's got all the Teamsters weeping on the set is probably coming out of the picture. Why? *It stops the show.* We're told less is more. This is a curious oxymoron, as it means more is better. But in film, *less* is always better. Tears are like homeopathic medicine: the smaller the dose, the greater the effect. And the timing of a gag, and so of a laugh, is the *essence* of the gag. And its timing will depend *on the way it is cut.* The folks on the set and the folks screening the dailies aren't seeing the thing cut and so should mistrust their reactions.

Nothing with a quill pen in it ever made a nickel. I think this is true, but it is, at very least, provocative. I myself don't respond to the Georgian in film and will addend a condign comment attributed to Harry Cohn. When head of Columbia, Mr. Cohn screened *One Million B.C.,* a cave drama with Victor Mature and Carole Landis, and remarked, "I can't vote for a film where the guy's tits are bigger than the broad's." A third film gem is the exhibitors' "Give me Tahiti in the winter and the Arctic in the summer"; all of which wisdom literature might be subsumed under the all-encompassing "Give 'em what they want."

Get out on your biggest laugh. And the aligned "Always leave 'em laughing" and "Always leave 'em wanting more." One should leave the theater thinking, "I never wanted it to end," rather than, "Now I am *sure* I've got my money's worth!" Nightclub performers had it: "When you *come* on, *be* on; and when you're done, get *off.*"

If you can't figure out what the scene's about, it's probably unnecessary. The process of organizing a film for shooting is called "boarding." A board is made up showing the scene number, the players, the physical elements (cars, stunts, effects, et cetera). The scene is identified both by number and by log line, a description of the scene just sufficient for its identification, e.g., Steve finds the map; Gramps falls downstairs.

I was preparing one movie and the unit production manager came over and politely pointed out that two of the scenes on the board had the same log line. "It isn't my place," she said, "but it occurred to me that maybe one of them was unnecessary." As, indeed, one was. A corollary of "If you can't figure it out" is "If it *is* necessary, it's necessary only once."

Always get an exit and an entrance. More wisdom for the director from the cutting room. The scene involves the hero sitting in a café. Dialogue scene, blah blah blah. Well and good, but when you *shoot* it, shoot the hero coming in and sitting down. And then, at the end, shoot him getting up and leaving. Why? Because the film *is* going to tell you various things about itself, and many of your most cherished preconceptions will prove false. The scene that works great on paper will prove a disaster. An interchange of twenty perfect lines will be found to require only two, the scene will go too long, you will discover another scene is *needed,* and you can't get the hero there if he doesn't get up from the table, et cetera.

Shoot an entrance and an exit. *It's free.*

I learned a corollary from John Sayles: at the end of the take, in a close-up or one-shot, have the speaker look left, right, up, and down. Why? Because you might just find you can get out of the scene if you can have the speaker throw the focus. To what? To an actor or insert to be shot later, or to be found in (stolen from) another scene. It's free. Shoot it, 'cause you just might need it.

I once designed a scene in a bookstore. Dialogue dialogue dialogue, blah blah blah. A later scene involved the hero coming back and reinterpreting the previous evidence he found there. On the day, I announced: "Wait a second, the *second* scene can be reduced to a mere insert" (shot of an object). I felt bold and was further emboldened by my strength in resisting all polite efforts to convince me to shoot the scene as previously written. "It's *free,*" I was told. "We're in the bookstore *anyway*" (shooting the first scene). No, I bravely announced. And then I had to come back after the film was cut and, at great expense and in healthy humiliation, shoot the scene as previously written. Why? I had offended the gods. My certainty in the face of polite reminders to accept the free shots had angered the powers that be. An attendant piece of film wisdom: "If enough people tell you you're dead, lie down."

What keeps them apart? (Billy Wilder) The engine of a love story is not what attracts them—we *know* that: they're young and pretty. The work should go into the construction of the plausible opposition to their union.

More wisdom from Billy Wilder, of the audience:

"Individually, they're idiots. Collectively, they're a genius."

Anyone who speaks of the audience's understanding as diminished has never had to make a living by appealing to them. If it's coherent, they *will* get it. The filmmaker's job is not to *pander* to them but to make his vision *coherent*.

Do not shoot the pretty girl's close-up last. For some reason, this very good advice is overlooked, and one *always* ends up shooting the pretty girl's close-up last thing in the day. This may be because the male leads are generally much more demanding, and they get the grease. Perhaps it is because the filmmaker, graciously putting himself in the same position as his audience, is in love with the pretty girl and feels he can count on her. Or maybe he'd just rather have her to look at at the end of a hard day. I don't know. One always ends up, as I have said . . .

My friend the soldier passed along a compendium of the wisdom of his racket. It, similarly, dripped with the, in his case, real rather than figurative, blood of experience: "When your plan of battle is proceeding perfectly, you have just walked into an ambush"; "All combat takes place at night, in the rain, at the intersection of four map segments"; "Never trust a recruit with a weapon or an officer with a map"; "If you can't remember which way the claymore is pointed, it is pointed at you"; "It is inadvisable to parachute into an area one has just bombed."

This mutual conjunction of the fatalistic and the mechanical, the mysterious and the mundane, confirms film as a true, if late-developing, human art. As such, its practice and contemplation connect us at once with both our most- and least-human aspects. Our ability to conceptualize about both the process and the product is accompanied, and inspired, by the pure animal joy of submersion in a mystery.

SOME PRINCIPLES

THE AUDIENCE; OR,
LESSONS FROM DUCK HUNTING

A duck decoy does not need to look like a duck.

It needs to look like a duck to a duck.

Wisdom, therefore, lies not in the phenomonological question "What does a duck look like?" but, rather, in the practical "What is a duck looking for?"

The duck, in this conceit, is our friend, the Audience, and I use the term "friend" advisedly.

Sun Tzu instructs, in his *Art of War,* to treat the opponent as if he were an employee—to ask, that is, what motivates him and to act accordingly.

The moviemaker, similarly, must treat the audience member not as an adversary but as an associate.

The untutored deal with an adversary by stealth, cunning, bribery, misdirection, blunt application of force—the tools, in short, of crime. And these are, of course, recognizable in their application by the film bureaucracy: the audience is bribed by promises of titillation, they are bombarded with endorsements from the cajoled or suborned, they are weakened by dulling repetitive advertisements, they are promised a glimpse of their favorite if they will behave (that is, attend), and so on.

The audience, knowing itself, thus, despised, reacts to films not as a legitimate entertainment but as a contest of will (one creates enmity by applying force; one may learn to prevail through understanding rather than strength—the basic tenet of jujitsu).

In using the tools of aggression and opposition, whether in Vietnam or in the calendar section of the newspaper, the aggressor strengthens the resolve of the opponent to resist, necessitating ever-greater prodigies of waste (bombing/advertisement) on the part of the powerful. Thus are the high brought low. One does not win the hearts and minds of a population by bludgeoning them.

But what if the audience were not an opponent to be bilked but a necessary adjunct of the process of creation, an associate whose needs, conscious and unconscious, the filmmakers strove to understand?

Let us return to our friend the duck.

The wealthy hunter might bespeak a decoy realistic to the nth degree. This decoy might be correct in every particular of size, form, and color, and yet the poor hunter in the next blind down might be attracting all the ducks with his roughed-out and unpainted decoy. Now, why is that?

Well, the poor man, unhampered by the capacity to waste, was forced to employ thought, and he wondered: What does a duck like? How does a duck *see*?

We have all had the experience of saying of a statue, "How lifelike," and, of a life mask, cast from the human form and painted to perfection, "How lifeless."

What was missing in the life mask? Life.

For the actual human being and the actual duck were created by, and so contain, a *mystery*. They cannot be reduced to mere measurements, and all attempts to do so (whether through the caliper of the decoy maker or through the audience testing of the social scientist) result in lifeless parody.

Life, in the art of the drama or of the carver, cannot be aped, and the attempt to remove the element of chance must doom the project absolutely. For another name for "chance" is "mystery," and another name is "art."

The artist carver, director, writer, or actor brings a (conscious or unconscious) understanding of the mystery of human interaction to his task.* And it is this ineffable element (*not* the mechanic verisimilitude) that attracts the audience. And it is this artistry that attracts the duck.

Just as the decoy cannot be all things to an incoming duck, the film cannot be all things to an audience. Better that it should be *some* thing, that it convey the desire of the filmmaker to tell a story rather than their desire to earn a living.

Most films are bad. They are, finally, just advertisements for themselves—elongated movie trailers, envisioned and cut with less skill than the trailer itself.

A good duck decoy, on the other hand, is a work of art and may be loved and admired in itself, on a tabletop, independent of its success in bringing home the game.

The films of De Sica, of Welles, of Michael Powell and Emeric Pressburger made little money and endure as spiritual delights.

On the other hand, there are films of which we, quite literally, *applaud the grosses,* while the films themselves are unwatchable (e.g., *Titanic*).

(There is a relationship of mutual exploitation fostered by the creation and marketing of the solely mercantile film. Someone said that the genius of the American tax code was that it turned everyone into a sneak and a criminal. Mass-market exploitation of the audience makes the producer and the viewer complicit in an adoration of wealth—the producer trying to mug the viewer, and the viewer submitting for the cheap thrill of the producer's notice. In this, the viewer is in the same

* As, indeed, does the inspired entrepreneur.

position as the star at the Oscars: he agrees to fawn and pant in return for a pat on the head. This is, of course, the reason for the Oscars' success as entertainment: the audience gets to see their oppressors brought low. It is like Boxing Day, when the lords of the manor had to pretend to serve the servants.)

There is another aspect to the hunting of the duck: The hunter whose poverty debars him from belief in the magical powers of the most expensive decoy (ad campaign, audience testing campaign, trailer, et cetera) must become a natural philosopher. He must teach himself to look at the totality of the situation. He may sit longer or stiller in the blind and so cultivate habits of patience, thought, and observation, perhaps, in the process, obtaining not only wisdom but also grace, as both his success and lack thereof may inspire him to a more profound understanding, so that not only his product but also his efforts achieve a sort of beauty that might be called art.

AESTHETIC DISTANCE

Charles Henry Parkhurst was a late-Victorian reformer. Like many who preceded and many who followed, his stock-in-trade was low-cost prurience. He haunted the dens of vice of Victorian New York City and wrote, at length, of their appalling, nay, demonic conditions.

The goodwilled people of that time, much like you and me, might read along, shaking their heads as they discovered the hoped-for mention of this or that preferred vice.

"Tsk tsk," they or you or I might say, as our eyes grew wide, our heart began to beat more insistently, and so on, increasing the urge to read.

For the newspaper, whatever its flag of convenience, exists to sell sex, gore, and outrage. Much like the movies.

In each, the moralistic tone is very much likely to enfold, and, indeed, to allow the sale of that denied to the high-minded. Most antiwar films succeed through the power of this engine. We viewers are titillated by images we are assured we have come to decry.

Not a Love Story, the 1981 Canadian documentary, passed as an exposé of the smut industry, but I suggest that, absent its odor of sanctity, it was powered by sexually explicit images and enjoyed by those who thought it good to watch the same.

The Green Mile, while purporting to be an indictment of

capital punishment, was a pictorial, inventive, extensive, and very graphic description of the same.

Can or could those above-named and unfortunate subjects be treated in a truly moral way? Of course. I will suggest, as for prostitution, Silvana Mangano in De Sica's *Gold of Naples* and, as for capital punishment, Stanley Kubrick's *Paths of Glory* or Daniel Mann's *I'll Cry Tomorrow*.

Each of these takes an essentially tragic tale and investigates it with dignity. Now, *Not a Love Story* and *The Green Mile* differ in degree. The second, a straightforward mercantile venture, adopts or accepts a degree of license offered by sanctimony. Why not? The first, *Not a Love Story,* sells flesh while it sails under the banner of exposé *toute entière,* to which a critic more moralistic than I might perhaps respond, "Shame on you."

Let us discuss *aesthetic distance.*

It is the goal of the dramatist to involve the audience in the working out of a hermetic syllogism.

The goal of the hero is stated, as are the impediments to that goal. The audience, then, engages its intellectual fantasies, attempting to anticipate the hero's possible solutions. This is called "getting involved." *Because* the creators have invested time and effort, they, the audience, become emotionally involved. They root for the hero, exult at his successes, are anxious for his triumph, and suffer at his reversals.

They are permitted to do so *in the degree that* the syllogism is plausible, solvable, simple, and clear.

Hamlet wants to find out who killed the king. All right, we'll play along. If Ringo can't get the sacred ring of Kali off his finger, he will be sacrificed. Ditto.

As we have signed on for what, in Hollywood, is known as "the ride," we identify with the hero (this is what the term means: that for the length of the drama, our interests are one).

The identified-with hero becomes an object of love (how

otherwise, as it is ourself?), and we want to know more about him.

The untutored mistake effect for cause. Their logical fantasy: that in the successful drama we want to know more about the hero, *therefore* a drama can be made successful by *telling* the audience more about him.

Now, the more the audience is told about the hero—the more their legitimate, indeed, induced desire is gratified—the less they care. For they have signed on to follow his journey in anticipation, glee, and dread. When the author indulges his ability to frolic away from the described path (the path, the *sole* path, to which the audience has vouchsafed its interest), the less interested the audience becomes.

(Canny test marketers hold "focus groups" at test screenings and quiz the audience on the film they've just seen. "What scenes did you like least?" Those in which the hero was in danger. "What character/s did you like least?" The villain. Oh, sigh.)

To return: the reductio ad absurdum of "we want to know more about him" is recourse to *actual* physical or biographical aspects *of the actor,* e.g., let's show his or her actual genitals, physical deformity, tattoo, et cetera; let's make reference to actual events in the actor's life that might excite interest.

This, while perhaps exciting audience interest *in general,* does so at the expense of audience interest *in the plot.* (Again, the author has thought it good to *detour* from that service for which we have paid and pledged our attention.)

This is called *violating the aesthetic distance.**

Cheap sentiment is indeed enduring. So is cheap scent.

---

* Steven Schachter's *Door to Door* (2002) stars William H. Macy as a man deformed by cerebral palsy. His goal is to become a door-to-door salesman. He *refuses* to let anything—including his diability—dissuade or divert him. The audience follows him in his goal and quits this most excellent film thinking the hero not a poor man but a hero.

THE FIVE-GAG FILM

The absence of affront at the violation of the aesthetic distance may be employed as a diagnostic tool indicating that the nature of the entertainment is not, *essentially,* dramatic.

Consider the use of the on-screen telephone number. The display of an actual telephone number on screen as part of a dramatic entertainment has been ruled legally actionable, as it may constitute invasion of privacy. Film and television have adopted for display the telephone exchange 555, which is never actually assigned and thus cannot incite the litigious. The nonoffending number, as we know, appears on the screen in instances such as this:

> BRENDA
> Sergeant Mulchahy, we have that important telephone number.

> SERGEANT MULCHAHY
> Give it to me, Brenda. . . .
> *(Brenda passes the sergeant a piece of paper on which we read "555-3948.")*

The audience is shown the number. Its display, however, does not aid but ruptures the dramatic flow; for the audience realizes that the number they have been shown, contrary to the assurances of Brenda, cannot be important either to her or to the sergeant, as it exists not to identify a telephone subscriber (suspect, victim, or indeed human being) but to dissuade vexatious litigation by viewers. This is called "violating the aesthetic distance."

Other examples of such violation follow.

An actor portrays a pianist. The actor sits down to play, and the camera moves, without a cut, to his hands, to assure us, the audience, that he is *actually playing*. The filmmakers, we see, have taken pains to show the viewers that no trickery has occurred, but in so doing, they have taught us only that *the actor portraying the part can actually play the piano*. This addresses a concern that we did not have. We never wondered if the actor could actually play the piano. We accepted the storyteller's assurances that the *character* could play the piano, as we found such acceptance naturally essential to our understanding of the story, but when the camera tilts down to the actor's actual fingers, we, in effect, experience *this:*

> **FILMMAKER**
> I'm going to tell you a story about a pianist.

> **AUDIENCE**
> Oh, *good:* I wonder what happens to her!

> **FILMMAKER**
> But first, before I *do,* I will take pains to reassure you that the actor you see portraying the hero *can actually play the piano.*

We didn't care till the filmmaker brought it up, at which point we realized that, rather than being told a story, we were being shown a demonstration. We took off our "audience" hat and put on our "judge" hat. We judged the demonstration conclusive but, in so doing, got yanked right out of the drama. The aesthetic distance had been violated.

So that's the aesthetic distance.

It is a name for that condition whose existence allows the audience to suspend its judgment (to, in effect, lower its guard) in return for receipt of a *specialized* experience.*

Deeply immersed in the drama—watching a great film, a work of art, *The Magnificent Ambersons* or *The Godfather* or, in a modern example, *Whale Rider,* the display of the telephone number 555- would be shocking indeed. How, we would rightly wonder, could such a wise storyteller make such an error? "We were *with* you . . . ," the saddened viewer might think. "Why did you trust us, and yourself, so little? Why have you ruined my ability to enjoy the fantasy?" (Jewish rabbinical tradition notes that adultery is like murder, for it is a crime that cannot be undone. Violation of the aesthetic distance is a rupture of the artist's compact with the audience, and, similarly, its rupture cannot be mended.)

Stunts in films similarly have a great capacity to rupture drama. They offer (in truth or in potential) a thrill, but that thrill may very well shatter the audience's agreement with the filmmaker.

More effective—and much more difficult—is the creation of a thrill by means that do *not* draw the audience's attention

---

* The psychoanalyst may, indeed, fall in love with the patient, and the two may conclude that indulgence in their overwhelming ardor excuses the doctor's violation of the role of analyst. All well and jolly, but the moment they start fooling around, the *special case* relaxation of societal norms (in this case regarding self-disclosure) that permitted the analysand to speak freely is revoked and the analysis is, effectively, over.

to but further enmesh the audience *in* the storytelling process, e.g., the surprise ending of *The Sixth Sense*. Here, the essential nature of the dramatic interchange—to engage the audience in *wondering what happens next*—is employed to lead them on to a surprising, inevitable, and, thus, thrilling conclusion.

The staged, self-contained stunt—or computer-generated event—on the other hand, offers the audience a treat, thus, as in the case of the amorous analyst and patient, gratifying their senses at the cost of destroying the special interchange.

Pornographic films, though availing themselves of the protective coloration of the drama, are merely a hemstitching together of events that, spectacularly, violate the aesthetic distance. But such violation in the porno film and in the pure "stunt" film (e.g., James Bond) neither shocks nor offends. The display of the 555- number, similarly, while it would rightly wrench us out of our immersion in an Akira Kurosawa film, goes unremarked in the summer skinflick or the effects blockbuster.

Our lack of disconnection, then, may be employed diagnostically. We may say that when the aesthetic distance has been violated but we, as viewers, feel no discomfort, the presentation we are viewing is not, strictly, a drama.

The pornographic film, we note, is not a drama. For although a pretext has been stated—a male and a female astronaut are stuck in a capsule in space and endeavor to get back to Earth—neither the characters nor the actors nor the audience cares about it. Everyone knows that they're just up there to copulate and that, after the required number of copulations, an acceptable device will be used to allow the astronauts to return to Earth, and the viewers to retain a scrap of self-respect.

The malfunction of the space capsule is not the basis of a plot. It is, in this film, a pretext. Similarly, the trend in comedy, of late, is toward the nondramatic. The early *Pink Panther* films all have a plot; *It's a Mad Mad Mad Mad World* has a plot; the Ealing comedies have a plot; the late spate of summer comedies have a pretext. They are, not unlike the porno film, a loose assemblage of (in this case) humorous effects or scenes. These hemstitched entertainments are not, per se, bad or indictable. Neither are they without precedent. Their antecedent, however, is not the drama but the circus.

The circus, the vaudeville, and, indeed, performance art please through the presentation of individually complete, intellectually empty effects (tricks, turns), such that the progress, one to the next, mimics the emotional journey undergone by the listener involved in the progression of an actual drama.

The work of arranging the circus, vaudeville, or burlesque turns in the best possible order is called "routining," a most revealing term meaning "optimally ordering the arbitrary."

Routining is, rightly, prized as a showbiz skill. One wants to close the circus with the quadruple somersault, not with the farting elephant. And much of the work of current film production—that passing as both screenwriting and directing—is essentially routining.

I believe that the enjoyment of the dramatic and the non-dramatic are *physiologically* different—that is, that different parts of not only the viewer's mind but of his *brain* are engaged in the two similar yet discrete experiences.

The dramatic experience is essentially *the enjoyment of the postponement of enjoyment*. The mouth waters at the prospect of a delicious meal; the palms sweat in anticipatory delight of sex. The enjoyment of the pseudodramatic entertainment has nothing to do with anticipation. It is, not only aesthetically but physiologically, akin to actual ingestion or congress.*

---

* Consider the difference between enjoyment and stimulation. One leaves the ballet feeling refreshed, as a promise has been fulfilled. One quits the video-game or pornographic film feeling empty and vaguely debauched—for one has

This is all well and good—as we see in the circus and pornography. And there's nothing wrong with film as compilation
(of gags, effects, slapstick). That the five-gag film has virtually
replaced the dramatically structured comedy is unfortunate,
however. For its success feeds the historical film-industry's loathing of any presentation necessitating delayed gratification—
which is to say, of drama.

---

only been stimulated. The brain, here, craves a *repetition of the stimulation,* as
with any drug. One may sit in front of the television for five hours, but after
King Lear one goes home.

BRINGING A GUN TO A KNIFE FIGHT; OR, A SHORT TOUR OF THE CONCEPT OF SUSPENSION OF DISBELIEF

It would be considered in questionable taste to demand a free dessert at the restaurant because one's aunt is dying of cancer. One commits the same solecism, however, in filming or presenting the affliction drama.

The talentless, misguided, or exploitative have long employed supradramatic devices in the construction of the drama, enlisting patriotism (see most any war movie) and right thinking (*Guess Who's Coming to Dinner,* et cetera), as these very human virtues, practiced in the wider world, are understood (subconsciously) by the viewer to trump an interest in mere entertainment.

"Do you appreciate this film, or do you hate the deaf/gays/blacks?" This is the (again, conscious or unconscious) mechanism of the issue drama.

The affliction drama (*Children of a Lesser God, The Shadow Box, Whose Life Is It Anyway?, Angels in America*) enlists the human capacity for sympathy and asks the sympathetic viewer to weep.

There's nothing wrong with a good cry (see most any film starring Bette Davis), but any claim to actual identity as a drama must rest upon the construction of a plot independent of the assignment of affliction to the protagonist.

Such a claim, like the demand for more pie, is plain bad manners.

Imagine, similarly, a candidate for office who asks for your vote because she is blind. "Yes," one might think, "that is certainly a shame, but I, the voter, pay taxes and so am entitled to representation. I will cast or withhold my vote according to my understanding of how this candidate's views reflect or inform my own; I fail to see how her affliction enters into this equation."

But we are biddable. The suspension of disbelief necessary to the dramatic transaction opens the door to its misuse by both the criminal and the well meaning.

As we enter the cinema, we relax our guard. We do so necessarily, because to resist, to insist on reality in the drama, is to rob ourselves of joy.

For who would sit through the cartoon thinking constantly, "*Wait* a second, *elephants can't fly!*"

Politicians (notably the right, in both America and Britain) have cannily understood this suspension of disbelief and have, since World War II, staged their political campaigns as *dramas,* with themes, slogans, inflammatory appeals, and villains.

This approach has put their opponents at an unfortunate disadvantage; for while the right is staging a thriller, their opponents are stuck presenting a lecture (the preferred tool of the left).

The ancient joke has a member of the majority culture taking a shortcut home through a dark alley in which he encounters a member of a despised minority. The minority fellow threatens the other with a knife, the proposed victim produces a revolver and says, "Isn't that just like a *(insert favorite racially derogatory term)* to bring a knife to a gunfight?"

Well, hijacking of the dramatic transaction is bringing a gun to a knife fight.

We are all at risk of victimization by inappropriate application of the dramatic mechanism.

Consider the Fuller brush salesman of yore. He knocked at

the door and said, "Good morning, Madam, which would you prefer today, our free brush or our free hand lotion?" The courteous and legitimately self-interested housewife opened the door to make her choice and found that, in so doing, she had made a commitment and entered into a dramatic interchange. The salesman had cleverly applied the human tropism toward friendliness, mixed it with that of greed, and his sale was made when and as the poor woman opened her door.

He had *suspended her disbelief*, circumventing her natural wariness of strangers, moving her past the trying initial encounter to a state wherein she magically (or dramatically) believed that, because of her unnamed excellences, she was to be the recipient of something for nothing.

She was flattered, bribed, and suborned through approach to her own legitimate friendliness. Game over. As were and are various happy victims of political bilge—"Recapture the dream," "It's morning in America," and my momentary favorite, "compassionate conservatism," a dramatic phrase enabling the subscriber to feel both superior and humble before God.

"Affliction drama" similarly, appeals to two of the viewer's weak spots: a desire to be politically responsible (or fashionable) and the intention to be compassionate. Overlooked in the transaction, however, is *the imaginary nature of the presentation*. The heroes, their desires, and their afflictions *are not real*. The viewer rewards himself for his compassion for a fictional victim. His compassion has cost him nothing; to the contrary, its exercise has been enjoyable—it was an entertainment.

The viewer here self-permitted an outpouring of emotion and endorsement that (he forgets) would be more problematical in the case of actual individuals.

Actual individuals are demanding, ungrateful, difficult to characterize or stereotype, combative, touchy, and easily offended (especially by unsolicited outpourings of sympathy). The actually ill display these behaviors to an increased extent.

Thus, the affliction drama turns the viewer into a sort of compassionate conservative, allowing him to believe he feels for the mass what he cannot feel for poor Aunt Sally: unlimited compassion, patience, and understanding.

GENRE

BANG-BANG

We humans love to kill. We therefore enjoy, both as fantasies and as histories, stories of murder.

We are particularly enamored of that fictive or nonfictive exploration of a "just war." What is a just war? It does not exist. War may be justifiable, but it cannot be just.

If the violence can be construed as just, our perverse entertainment is less despicable. Our enshrinement of the Greatest Generation is an attempt to co-opt what we, their descendants, perceive as their license to kill. "Just" is not a description of a war but of our enjoyment of its contemplation.

Any actual contact with violence, however, creates an abhorrence of violence.

Ex-fighters, ex-police officers, and ex-soldiers are notable for their lack of belligerence; to the contrary, those displaying arrogance or combativeness have generally never experienced or seen actual violence—their belligerence masks their fear and displays their ignorant belief that battles are somehow won by intimidation.

Violent encounters are won only by those putting themselves at risk of violence.

Though a true hero does so, the audience does not. They, thus, enjoy what they perceive as a real thrill of victory without risk.

This is the attraction of the war movie, and its pervasive influence has infected and perverted American foreign policy (vide a noncombatant president who sends young men into combat by quoting a cinematic taunt: "Bring it on"—cf. "Make my day").

The illusion of impunity has pervaded our national conflicts since Korea—as if it were possible to prevail against a foreign country without killing and being killed. The misconceived antisepsis of the Vietnam air war, of Grenada, of Iraq I and II reveals a view of impunity like that of the moviegoer.

The viewer is presented with this paradigm: The hero (i.e., you, the viewer, whom he represents) is *good*. The hero will undergo various struggles in which you, the viewer, will be able to vicariously enjoy his stoicism while undergoing no pain. Your desire to do violence will be pandered to by an incontrovertible presentation of the justice of the hero's cause and by a (ritual) period of initial restraint on his part.

This false glow of untried and (in the case of the moviegoer) proxy triumph is the drug of the bully. It seduces the weak-minded and emboldens the arrogant.

Murder has, of course, always been a staple theme of the dramatist. Its mythologic exploration is cathartic, e.g., *The Scottish Play, The Iliad, Crime and Punishment,* and, in fact, *Paths of Glory, The Ox-Bow Incident, A Place in the Sun.* These are not advertisements for, but warnings against, violence. As such they are cleansing. They artistically exhibit, they reveal and *acknowledge,* the human capacity for evil. By so doing they strip from the viewer the burden of repression.

The fiction: "I am good, I am incapable of violence, and even if I were capable of violence, I know for a fact that my cause would be just and, further, that *as* it is just, my crime would have no psychological (let alone criminal) consequences." This is the drug offered by the violent film. It represses human feelings of rage and our shame at them. It is an opiate of which increasingly larger doses must be taken for increasingly smaller effect. Its effect is anesthetic.

The O. J. Simpson show-trial was a corruptive entertainment. The probity, the careful and decent aversion of interest necessary in a civil society, were replaced with the lurid, insatiate need for retelling what the viewing audience quickly forgot was an actual human tragedy.

Reaction to the verdict split, in the United States, largely along racial lines: the whites appalled, the blacks content.

This was a political reaction: White juries had, for centuries, dismissed open-and-shut cases of white assaults on blacks. White police, defense lawyers, and prosecutors historically colluded to enforce apartheid in the criminal courts. So blacks content with an absurd verdict, the colors of the major players switched, was and is understandable. White rage and depression at the verdict were, to a large extent, compounded not by incredulity but, in fact, by an *understanding* (conscious or unconscious) of the black point of view: white society had just been mugged by the same vicious, transparent mechanism that it had immemorially employed against blacks.

Whites had been asked: "How do you like it now?" And they were forced to answer, "Not at all."

Similarly, Americans, white and black, may get all puffed out and happy at war films—the recruiting posters of the forties, *Back to Bataan;* the rather Stalinist patriotism of the cold war, *Retreat, Hell!* and *Strategic Air Command.* But notice the discrepancy between our enjoyment of this merchandising of violence and our lack of glee at the body bags of Vietnam and, now, of Iraq.

The unfortunate and inevitable concomitant of "Bring it on" is "How do you like it now?"

THE COP MOVIE

The paramilitary fantasy, dating from *Dr. No* (1962), is one of omnipotence; the superhero is unbeatable, possessed of all skills and knowledge. He may (and in the drama, of course, must) find himself in peril at stated intervals, but this peril exists only as contrast for his eventual and inevitable triumph.

The techno-thriller reduces what is essentially an automaton even further: these books (and, to a slightly lesser extent, the movies based on them) concern the primacy of *machines*.

The human protagonists of these dramas—e.g., *The Terminator, The Matrix, The Bourne Identity*—are barely human. Having no discernible feelings or desires, they are in effect machines. As the protagonist of the drama must be, in our understanding, ourself, we see here the childhood wish for certainty in its ultimate state: a wish not to feel, to be a machine.

The idea of the affectless hero (hero-as-machine) seems to date from the close of World War II, Isaac Asimov's sad robots, the *Joe Gall* books of Philip Atlee, Donald Hamilton's *Matt Helm* series, and the James Bond books. Here we see a sort of cultural autism. Western society, overloaded by the events of the preceding forty years, reimagines itself (in its hero) as uninvolved. It is not that we are incapable of emotions but that we do not *require* them.

James Bond may have sex but not love. Clint Eastwood's character name, the Man with No Name, speaks for itself.

Dirty Harry, like most of the franchise thrillers, features a protagonist who is not only autistic but also sociopathic—that is, licensed (in James Bond's case, by the state; in that of the Man with No Name, by his personality) to commit murder. These films not only license but also laud the conscienceless state. (We see their progeny in today's computer games, which are not, traditionally, games at all, but, effectively, psychological biofeedback machines, training the mind away from inherited or acquired compunction.)

The police adventure is different. It is a treatment not of the absence of emotion but of the presence repression.

Where the paramilitary film plays out the infantile power fantasy—the infant, denied the breast, is deprived and wants to kill the offending world—the police drama plays out the rather more elaborated manipulations of the youngster confronting society.

The adolescent or preadolescent is at war not with the world but with his parents. His mutually exclusive needs for support and for freedom seem incapable of happy resolution, and this impossibility tortures him. He, like the rogue cop, withdraws or is temporarily expelled from the police department—the repressive organization. He is called back for one more case and, in attempting its solution, is forced to resolve the *underlying* cause of disruption. That cause is revealed to be not his behavior, in any given instance, and not the supposed "crime" (for, psychologically, he, the hero, and we, the viewer, must know *himself* to be the perpetrator) but his *relationship to his parents.*

Put differently, the hero cop—the adolescent—is called back not to find a murderer but to acknowledge the final necessity of a break with the juvenile figures of authority.

His feelings are eventually validated as he finds, inevitably, that the real crime is not that perpetuated by the criminal but the *corruption of his superiors,* who have colluded in its commission or in its cover-up (e.g., *Bullitt, The Detective, Training Day*). Only by discovering their corruption (that is, their frail humanity) can he cease fighting with them and so depart—which is to say, mature—in peace.

The last reel of the police drama clarifies the problem: it is not that evil exists but that the hero/viewer has an insufficiently developed mechanism for dealing with it. The world will not be *cleansed* by the hero's triumph, but he, himself, will be free. Of what? Of the constant necessity of conscious service to the repressive mechanism.

Vide: at the end of most canonical police dramas, the hero leaves his organization (e.g., *Serpico, Prince of the City, Three Days of the Condor, Spy Game*). The form of these autonomically created dramas of renunciation springs full blown from our unconscious—as does the phrase "What seems to be the trouble, Officer?"

In these, the hero, like Oedipus, called to find the cause of the city's unrest, finds it in the astounding but inevitable place. In Oedipus it is himself (a tragedy); in the police drama it is his revered superiors (a drama). Having found it, the hero is free to retire from his vocation—in grief or sorrow—to an independent life.

Stanislavsky wrote that drama stands in the same relationship to melodrama as tragedy does to comedy—that is, that tragedy is not heightened drama but heightened comedy. Here, in the perhaps special case of the cop movie, we have drama that might be tragedy manqué. In the denouement the burden of repression is lifted (as in comedy) but only at the cost of its replacement by sorrow.

FILM NOIR AND HE-MEN

I am just returned from San Francisco.

As a besotted movie lover, I cannot, of course, drive those streets without thinking of the car chase in *Bullitt*.

I meditate on the direction in this sequence and the beautiful, protracted airport chase that closes the film.

This is tough, concise, and, if I may, butch moviemaking, and I love it.

I think of Peter Yates's other crime films, *Robbery* and *The Friends of Eddie Coyle*. Two smashing films noirs—all bad guys fighting for the swag, for their lives, in a world without rules—blunt, perfect filmmaking.

My reverie shifts to another of my favorite truly tough films, *Point Blank,* and thence to another of John Boorman's films, *Deliverance*. These films are *dark*. And, it occurs to me, they're all directed by Brits.

Is the British sensibility, I wonder, more suited to the production of film noir?

Film noir is the conjunction of violence and irony, and we Americans don't do irony very well. We are a straightforward and self-righteous people, so we are rather good at viciousness and humor but lacking in irony.

Americans Stanley Kubrick, Cy Endfield, and Jules Dassin turned out some smashingly ironic stuff *(The Killing, Dr.*

Strangelove, Zulu, Night and the City, Rififi), but they, of course, ended up—by choice or as fugitives from American fury (the House Un-American Activities Committee)—as expats in Britain. Perhaps being bombed at regular intervals throughout the twentieth century has given the British a different slant on the entertainment quotient of violence.

British war films—*In Which We Serve, The Cruel Sea, One of Our Aircraft Is Missing,* indeed, Cy Endfield's magnificent *Zulu*—stress unity rather than, as in American films, a confected competition *between* comrades under arms.

Most American World War II films feature interunit antagonisms: the drill instructor vs. the recruit *(Sands of Iwo Jima),* the commander vs. the passed-out subordinate *(Run Silent, Run Deep),* the boss vs. the flyers *(Twelve O'Clock High),* two guys battling for the same girl *(Bombardier).*

This plot can also be found in *They Gave Him a Gun; The D.I.; Retreat, Hell!; Sergeant York;* and so on. It is, schematically, the essence of most American war films. The prize attendant upon the conflict's eventual resolution is (for the protagonists and the audience) the license to fight the actual enemy—in effect, to engage in violence. (Cf. American foreign policy, wherein, at this writing, the combat reluctant are branded by the administration as traitorous—or, at best, as misguided—and the reward for the individual's or the country's overcoming its abhorrence or reluctance to battle is a "good clean" fight.)

The cleansing (if false) reduction of the American war film is "conquer we must, if our cause is just" and that of our gangster film is "crime does not pay"—two equally debatable propositions.

Your British gangster films are more involved with how-to and, to this amateur of the ironic, therefore rather more enjoyable. They deal not with misguided souls but with actually-not-very-nice people.

This is a great film tradition, and I cite *The Blue Lamp; Robbery; Peeping Tom; The Long Good Friday; Sexy Beast; Mona Lisa; The Krays; Lock, Stock and Two Smoking Barrels; Snatch; Croupier;* and Mike Hodges's *I'll Sleep When I'm Dead.*

This last film is notable for its almost complete absence of narration—a writer's dream and a moviegoer's delight. For the absence of narration leaves only the *narrative.* We watch in order to discover who the folk are, what might be their relationship, what they want, and how they are going to go about getting it.

I particularly recommend the film's protagonist, Clive Owen, in his personification of enigma.

Speaking of casting, *Circle of Danger* (1951) is a British postwar drama. In it, Ray Milland's brother has died as a member of a Special Boat Service wartime assault. Milland cannot make sense of the reports of the circumstances of his brother's death. He suspects foul play and goes to England to investigate. He finds, one by one, the surviving members of his brother's squad.

All clues indicate that the solution to the mystery lies in one Sholto Lewis, the leader of the commando squad and, as per the interviewed squad members, "the bravest man who ever lived."

Milland finally finds an address for Douglas. He rings, and the door is opened by Marius Goring. Mr. Goring is togged out in ballet gear. He opens the door in tights, a cashmere sweater jauntily tied around his neck, his feet in a very good fourth position. In the background we see the dance rehearsal that Milland's ring has interrupted.

Mr. Goring gives Milland something of a moue and says, "Yes?"

Milland: "I'm looking for Sholto Douglas."

Goring: "I'm Sholto Douglas. Bad casting, eh?"

I love the British cinema. My idea of perfection is Roger
Livesey (my favorite actor) in *The Life and Death of Colonel
Blimp* (my favorite film) about to fight Anton Walbrook (my
other favorite actor). In the great dueling scene between the
two, Livesey is asked by the referee if he is skilled in the saber.
He replies, "I think I know which end to hold."

Other examples of British restraint: I give you Celia Johnson in *In Which We Serve* making a speech to the force that
robs her and her friends of their husbands, their ship ("I give
you the *Torrant*," she says, simply—no "show," just perfection); Elsa Lanchester in *Rembrandt,* facing down the bailiffs
("And *that's* the *law* in *Holland* . . . "); Alec Guinness going
mad in *Tunes of Glory;* Stanley Holloway in the train station
in *Brief Encounter;* the slavey in *Cavalcade* ("I know where
Africa is on a *map;* where is it *really* . . . ?")

In George MacDonald Fraser's magnificent war memoir,
Quartered Safe Out Here, he writes of an infantry assault
across open country. He looks at his platoon advancing de-
terminedly into enemy fire and says his only thought was
". . . Englishmen."

Or, in the terms of my particular métier: hold the emotion,
thanks; we understand.

The attitude has been tagged as stoicism, but perhaps
it's just professionalism—why not let the *audience* have the
experience?

Perhaps those of us who live surrounded by emotion—
doctors, police, lawyers, dramatists—are not much moved by
the emotional. I know I'm not. I prefer the clean statement to
the plea, the film noir to the gangster film. And, if you will
grant me that segue, I will continue.

The gangster film is a sentimental look at the world of
crime. There are, we are told, *good* bad criminals; there is a
code of honor; there is either justice or accountability. This is
a film as written by a criminal, which is to say, a sentimental,

self-servicing, pleasant lie. The film noir, on the other hand, depicts a cold Darwinian zero-sum world, a world without rules and without judgment. A film, if you will, written by a cop.*

I prefer the film noir.

The French, too, have, of course, had their innings, with *Bob le Flambeur, Rififi, Wages of Fear, Daybreak* (now, there's a film that just ain't kidding); and permit me to name our American *Gun Crazy* (the original) and various other black-and-white poverty row (the historical precursor of the independent film) works: *Detour, The Narrow Margin, Dillinger, The Rise and Fall of Legs Diamond, Plunder Road, Quicksand, Kiss the Blood Off My Hands,* and *T-Men.*

The American film noir grew out of postwar despair and a lack of funding on the part of the despairing. These films featured extended sequences shot on the side of a desolate road—no sets, little lighting, just great acting and a great script.†

Aristotle cautions that it is insufficient for the hero to get the idea. Many modern moviemakers, however, act as if they hadn't read his book. Their films depict the gentle progress of the protagonist toward self-actualization—usually depicted as a slow, arms-extended twirling on a beach (as if the expression of a racial memory of our descent from the shipworm).

Not the film noir. Vide *Point Blank,* where we have Lee Marvin, at the jump, robbed, shot, and left for dead on a deserted island. This fellow doesn't want self-actualization, he wants blood. And Sterling Hayden in *The Killing* wants *the money.*

The Killing is, I believe, the world's greatest film noir. The traditional subgenre here is "one last job."

---

* There is a long close affinity between writers and cops; we share the sad knowledge that everyone is always lying.
† A traditional recipe for genius: inspiration, a plan, not enough time.

Kubrick's team for the one last job is the greatest compilation of tough talent known to man: Ted de Corsia as the crooked cop; Elisha Cook Jr. in his perennial (and perennially brilliant) turn as the weak link; Joe Sawyer as the bartender with the ailing wife; Kola Kwariani as the ex–wrestling champion of the world; Timothy Carey as the shooter; Marie Windsor (cf. *The Narrow Margin*) as the loose-wheel bad girl who takes down the job; Jay C. Flippen as the bankroll, in love, into the bargain, with Sterling Hayden; Vince Edwards as Marie's killer boyfriend.

None of these people would tug at a heartstring to save his life. Or, to put it differently, they can be trusted.

I got to make a heist film with Gene Hackman. Like many of the stars in the above-instanced works, he is an actual tough guy. (Lee Marvin was a marine commando in the Pacific, Hayden in the Adriatic, et cetera.) Hackman was a China marine, race-car driver, stunt pilot, deep-sea diver.

These men, and their performances, are characterized by the *absence of the desire to please*. On screen, they don't have anything to prove, and so we are *extraordinarily* drawn to them.

They are not "sensitive"; they are not antiheroes; they are, to use a historic term, "he-men." How refreshing.

There will always be the same number of movie stars.

There is a table of operations, and the places must be filled. As with politicians, irrespective of the distinction of the applicant pool.

But I vote for the tone of a less sentimental time.

Look at the photographs in the family collection, of Dad or Grandad during the war or the Depression. We see individuals captured in an actual moment of their lives, not portraying themselves for the camera. I used to look at them and think one didn't see those faces today. We saw them—briefly—on September 11.

SHADOW OF A DOUBT

I should like to add to my film noir and he-men screed *Shadow of a Doubt* by that great American Alfred Hitchcock.

This, I believe, is Hitchcock's finest film. At the risk of sounding like a film student, I will refer to the construction of the shots, than which one could find no better exemplar in all of film. We have no stone lions rearing up, nor that baby carriage found in *Battleship Potemkin* (in a prescient adumbrage to Brian De Palma's 1987 *The Untouchables*). Arguably, the feat in *Shadow* is even more praiseworthy than that of Eisenstein—for Hitchcock is shooting only that to which he referred derisively as mere "pictures of people talking."

The movie is a sick and magnificent treatment of sexual abuse. It is coded as a story of a killer returned to his sister's home.

Charles, the villain (Joe Cotten), woos, marries, and kills rich widows. He comes back to Santa Rosa, posing as a retired industrialist, to live with his sis and her two daughters. The older, Charlotte, is called Charlie in honor of her uncle.

The two Charlies have a secret. She discovers that he is not what he seems, and her threats to tell are countered by his threats, first to discredit her, then to allow her to tell and so "break her mother's heart."

He proceeds to try to kill her by various stratagems, and in the last twenty seconds, she turns the tables on him, and he falls to his death in front of the oncoming train that was to've brought her demise.

Throughout the film, Cotten is standing too close and speaking too syrupily to the nubile, inevitable Teresa Wright, America's good girl.

She is first honored, then charmed, and, then, little by little, gets hep to the jive. And Hitchcock designs each sequence magnificently. There is no "master, over, close-up" about it. Each sequence is designed around its particular theme and purpose in the unfolding story. One could easily label them, e.g., alarm, suspicion, second thoughts, challenge, remorse. It may be the world's best silent film, undiminished even by the addition of dialogue.

Why are silent films potentially better?

The perfect film is the silent film, just as the perfect sequence is the silent sequence. Dialogue is inferior to picture in telling a film story. A picture, first, as we know, is worth a thousand words; the juxtaposition of pictures is geometrically more effective. If a director or writer wants to find out if a scene works, he may remove the dialogue and see if he can still communicate the idea to the audience.

Ancient theological wisdom put it thus: "Preach Christ constantly—use words if you must."

RELIGIOUS FILMS

Religious films have as much of a chance of increasing humane behavior as *Porgy and Bess* had of ending segregation. Religious films have but two subcategories: sappy and exploitative.

In the first, good things happen to good people. The heroes in this film have gone a little bit astray: they are dismissive to their inferiors or brusque with their children. An angel shows up, and all is put aright, cf. *A Christmas Carol, It's a Wonderful Life, The Bishop's Wife, Here Comes Mr. Jordan, Miracle on 34th Street.*

I list the above as religious films, as each is driven by the engine of belief in human benignity. We leave the theater thinking, "Well, I guess maybe we humans aren't such a bad lot after all." These films employ variations on the Santa Claus myth of godhood, that is, they borrow a biblical model of apotheosis, cleanse it of terror and awe, and present it as light-hearted entertainment.

The second subcategory is the straight-up or out-of-the-closet religious film, those endeavoring to depict mythical, historical, or doctrinal aspects of a specific religion—*The Robe, Ben-Hur, The Ten Commandments, The Last Temptation of Christ, The Passion of the Christ*—attempting to awaken or reengage the enthusiasm of the faithful.

These films professing fealty to received religion are, most literally, preaching to the choir, the reductio ad absurdum of "based on a true story."

But "based on a true story" is a come-on, the aesthetic equivalent of "no loan request refused."

For, at best, the creator has fashioned a film based on his understanding, interpretation, and reduction of the report of an actual occurrence. But just as it is impossible to utter a statement without inflection, it is impossible to make a film that is free of interpretation.

To claim artistic impunity, therefore, because of the sanctity of the source material is, perhaps, disingenuous.

The audience does not care if the film is based on a true story, only if it *is* a true story.

To invoke the sacrosanct is also the best trick of our friends the politicians: "Would you want your sister to marry one?" (defense of segregation); "Marriage is the backbone of civilization" (opposition to gay marriage).

In the heat of the theatrical moment, whether in the theater or the convention center, we can become enraptured to the point where we forget that our sister is going to marry whomever she wishes. And that our uncle Fred, our mother, or, indeed, we ourselves, may be as gay as possible, and that civilization nonetheless seems to continue stumbling along.

The power of iconography is such that it can endorse, and in fact exult, psychotic savagery *(Triumph of the Will)* or, devoid of content, convince an audience into thinking they have actually seen a film *about* something *(Forrest Gump)*.

Neophyte, incompetent, or bored filmmakers *show* those things they cannot dramatize, e.g., a slow pan over the heroine's desk: "Look, here are photos of her kayaking with her children, a copy of *The Theory of the Leisure Class,* a bronzed hockey skate, and a cased butterfly. She must be an interesting person."

The dramatic biographer is given a set of facts; but he, no less than the "documentary" recorder of the desktop, is still charged with making a choice. And whether charged or not, *is* making a choice.

Just as the cataloguer must decide if the kayaking photo or the hockey skate is seen first, is better lit, is closer to the camera, or "prettier," so the biographer must not only choose the facts to depict but also order and interpret them, weighing the reliability, honesty, authenticity, and possible bias not only of himself but of the original reporter(s).

This task is somewhat complicated when the source material is, to the filmmaker, holy writ.

The job of the viewer, here, is also more complicated: To what extent does civility require a nonbeliever to withhold judgment of a statement of faith not his own? To what extent must an adherent shelve aesthetic considerations in favor of an endorsement of his faith? And what if, God forbid, a religious film were to contain material actually derogatory to another faith and/or race? Would it be sufficient for the filmmaker to point to literature sacred to him but offensive to others and shrug, "What can I do? It's holy writ"?

It is written that whoever grasps the Torah without its covering will die, which the sages interpret to mean that even, and perhaps especially, holy writ may be destructive if the individual does not recognize his responsibility for interpretation: Christian tradition renders this as "The letter kills but the spirit frees."

For, just as with the placement of the hockey skates, our human mind is incapable of uncolored perception, let alone transmission. Interpretation, in the artist and in the viewer, is always and inevitably taking place, and the more the creator is aware of this, the better able both he and the viewer will be to seek out the *essential* truth of a story.

On which note, America, ever the entertainer, is currently being roiled and churned about the handy topic of gay marriage. A Massachusetts Democrat, the first openly gay member of Congress, was speaking to his constituents in a fishing town on the coast. Newly out, he was braving the puritan wrath of those who had elected him. One outraged soul asked if he was unaware that the Bible said, *explicitly,* that it was an abomination for one man to lie with another. The congressman asked if the constituent was unaware that the Bible used the same language about the eating of shellfish.

Movies possess unlimited power to entertain. They have, however, no power whatever to teach. The audience lends its attention only for the purpose of entertainment and will deny (consciously or unconsciously) its attention to any other purpose. (The child wants his bedtime story—it is an impertinence to use it as a lecture.)

But there is little in life more entertaining than self-righteousness and self-affirmation; occasionally, therefore, we find a film claiming to advance or depict a doctrine that some may find incontestable, indeed, holy, but that to others is pernicious.

Adherents, whether they know it or not, go to see these films *to be entertained.* (The correct venue for religious devotion is the holy place, not the cinema; and communion with the divine, whether the kiddush of the Jews or the Communion of the Catholics, is better celebrated with the traditional bread and wine than with popcorn and Coca-Cola.)*

Did *Taxi Driver* inspire John Hinckley Jr. to attempt assassination?

---

* The power of the doctrinal film consists in the ability of the doctrine in this venue and depiction to reaffirm or, unfortunately, to enrage—both entertaining emotions and inappropriate to the confines of the cinema.

We know that *The Birth of a Nation,* in its bold statement of the "unfortunate truth" that Negroes are inferior, helped endorse the rebirth of the Ku Klux Klan, and that *Triumph of the Will* helped to enthuse the Nazis.

It is, I think, the responsibility of filmmakers and distributors to assess the potential impact of their wares on those who might just mistake entertainment for exegesis, and for license.

A helpful counterexample is Joseph Goebbels's commendation of the SS: that history will record that they were capable of doing these terrible things without losing their essential humanity.

THE SEQUEL

My eight-year-old wanted to go see the sequel, so we schlepped out of the house and over to the movie theater.

The original had by no means been bad. It was intermittently funny and generally good-natured. The sequel, however, was an obscenity. How, I wondered, was it possible to make a film that bad?*

If a comedy has one hundred gags in it, one might predict that, say, three of them might be raucous, ten more pretty funny, thirty on top of that somewhat diverting, and all at the very least recognizable as an attempt to amuse.

But this sequel, this part two of a tremendously successful comedy, was not funny at all.

Not only were there no laughs, there were no premises identifiable as *intended to produce laughs*.

---

* I was reminded of the studies in parapsychology conducted at Duke University some years back. These famous Rhine experiments made bold to plumb the hidden powers of the mind. The paired subjects were given various flash cards blazoned with a star, a crescent, a box, a circle, then separated and asked to concentrate on the identity of the card their opposite number held. Professor Rhine found no positive correlation between the cards and the guesses. That is, the diviner could not guess correctly a percentage of times greater than predictable as random.

But wait. On review, Rhine found several instances where the *wrong* guesses far surpassed the predictable norm.

(That is, given five icon cards, a random selection must be correct approxi-

I was put in mind of contemporary American political style, in which whether or not the will of the people is subverted, it is not even mollified.

As voters, and as cinemagoers, we have agreed, as it were, to be wooed. We know we deserve to be met at our flat, perhaps given a corsage, before we step out.

But here is a concupiscent lout at our doorstep, his member in his hand, and he proclaims, "Later on, perhaps I'll buy you a sandwich. Now hike up your skirts."

"But," I say, "*but* were we, the despoiled populace, not historically entitled to a little bit of nicety, a bit of circus with our stale bread, a fine turn of phrase, at the very least?"

How about, at least, a mouthable slogan—"Remember the *Maine*," or "Fifty-four Forty or Fight," or "No Taxation without Representation"?

Sure, the practice of the big lie has distinguished provenance (cf. the Crusaders' cry, "Hep," an acryonym meaning *Jerusalem est perdita;* "Remember the Belgian Orphans"; and the historical romance *Wag the Dog,* to name but a few). But we ship our sons off to kill or be killed for reasons that are incapable of explanation, and we do not receive in return even an acceptable bumper sticker.

It need not even be rousing—it need but be identifiable as an *honest attempt to incite* (cf., again, "Gosh, you look pretty tonight"). The swain wants to get his leg over. The oligarchy wants to rob everyone blind. Of course they do, and of course they *shall*. But wouldn't a concern for simple good manners suggest they proceed in an approved and respectful fashion?

And the motion picture megaliths, having earned more money than they could have foreseen with the original, begin

---

mately 20 percent of the time. The greater the number of attempts, the more closely the correct guesses must approach 20 percent. If one guesses one thousand times and is correct only 10 percent of the time, some force other than the operations of chance must be at work.)

eating their own entrails in a frenzy to earn all the rest of the money with the sequel. And they collude and scheme and test and confab to make sure that *each* moment of the film is recognizable as that moment that should take place at that time, in a sequel to a film whose franchise is so important that *nothing* must be risked that might endanger its success.

Professor Rhine might watch the film, as did I, in wonder. It contains not one moment of jollity, humor, or respect for the audience that paid for their inclusion. How hard those executive, associate, cosupervising, and coexecutive producers must have labored to create a product bearing no trace whatever of the human.

They, those producers, had made themselves pure and cleansed their work of the accidental, the frivolous, the whimsical. Those qualities, in film one, had made them rich, and now those qualities, like the proverbial first wife, have gone to the wall. And like the first wife, they will not return.

Jewish law states that there are certain crimes that cannot be forgiven, as they cannot be undone. It lists murder and adultery. I add this film.

That same night my wife and daughter and I watched *I Know Where I'm Going!* This film by Powell and Pressburger (1945) is one of the world's great love stories and my wife's favorite film.

A young woman from the London beau monde is en route to a Scottish isle to marry sir somebody or other, a wealthy, et cetera. A storm strands her on Mull, some few miles' sail from her destination. She meets MacNeil, poor Lord of Killoran (her intended isle); they fall in love. They are kept apart by her indecision. They eventually brave the storm to sail to Killoran, are almost drowned, and return to Mull, where they are, thank God, united for all time.*

---

* Obiter dicta: (1) Pride goeth before a fall. (2) MacNeil, Lord of Killoran, was originally to be played by Laurence Olivier. He was replaced, at the last

"For all time," in this case, having lasted every moment of the more than sixty years viewing by delighted moviegoers. Pressburger, an Eastern European Jew, creates the perfect fantasy of Scotland, as Warner, Fox, Laemmle, Mayer, and Goldwyn, European Jews, created the fantasy of America. But this perhaps exceeds the brief of this essay.

---

moment, by Roger Livesey. Livesey was performing onstage during the shooting of *I Know Where I'm Going!* He commuted daily from London to Shepperton Studios, and the whole of his performance, supposedly shot on the Isle of Mull, is either on a studio set or against rear-screen projections. The long shots, taken in Scotland, feature a photo double. (3) The Rhine experiments at Duke were largely discredited when it was found that two of the prime subjects were confidence people who were cheating like mad.

PASSING JUDGMENT

REVERENCE AS OPPOSED TO LOVE

One of the great cinematic delights of the sixties was the animated short *Bambi Meets Godzilla.*

For those who have not been blessed, a young, scampering Bambi crests a hill and looks winningly to the right and left. He raises his ears, sensing danger. A huge billion-ton monster, Godzilla, comes over the hill and stomps Bambi into preserves. Roll credits.

Here is my own B vs. G story.

I was at a show business party the other day, and a friend expressed a rather egregious opinion. We all, being herd creatures, recoiled; she shrugged and said that she had grown old and one of the chief delights of aging was the ability to say whatever one thought. This was the second time in two days I had heard the phrase. The French, onetime ally of America, say, "jamais deux sans trois," so I must assume that this phrase, "age and express yourself," has been in the air around me for some time and that I have just become aware of its presence.

Why would that be? I wonder, and the answer swims to the forefront of my consciousness. I have grown old.

Having grown old, I will search for prerogatives and exercise them.

I need not believe the drivel that is spoken around me—

I feel lighter already—such wistful submission has only ever earned me increased grief, and I am free to *speak my own*. I can say whatever I want, as per the sibyl of the party. I need not tell the transparent lie to avoid the wretched dinner and so on.

There are, of course, limits. The Constitution of the United States, that lovely document, draws the line at advocating violent overthrow of the government, and the usage of the British Isles has an unwritten caveat barring criticism of Laurence Olivier.

But I just can't take it anymore, and I will, like Ayn Rand's Atlas, shrug the now intolerable burden.

I can't stand Laurence Olivier's acting. He is stiff, self-conscious, grudging, coy, and ungenerous. In *Khartoum,* the whole world, Arab and Christian, refers to *his character* as the Mahdi, while he, covered in chocolate and with a false nose the size of Dorsetshire, refers to himself gutturally, as the "MACCH-di," as if to correct the pronunciation of those, fedayeen or thespian, one would have supposed to have been his colleagues.

In *That Hamilton Woman,* he whispers and turns his face from the camera throughout; in *49th Parallel,* who knows *what* the deuce he is doing, other than turning in what I believe to be the only truly bad performance in any Powell and Pressburger film. He has a moment, as Hurstwood in *Carrie,* when Dreiser's safe swings closed, and is not bad in the musician scenes as Archie Rice in *The Entertainer.* But, in general, I'm hungry for lunch, and all he's serving is an illustrated menu.

This is not to detract from his status as the world's greatest actor. He won that position fairly, kept it honorably, and contributed to the British, and to the world, theater. And those who saw him onstage speak of him with reverence. But the good he did, I say, aside: We speak of the art and artists who move us not with reverence but with love. And I cannot love Olivier's performances.

Who, then, will I class against him? What shibboleth, you wonder, will I list to augment your umbrage?

Here I pause and imagine that you have beaten me to the punch and have correctly deduced that I am about to report my love for Tony Curtis.

You may snort with contempt and recall his Brooklynese, "Yonda stands da castle of my faddah." But I will name, in support, but two of his performances. To the mention of the first you will all smile with love; those who know the second will nod sagely in agreement:

Some Like It Hot and *The Boston Strangler.*

The first is the *perfect* comic turn. As the first beleaguered, then besotted (with Marilyn Monroe) saxophone player, he is, as we say, "as clean as a hound's tooth." He plays low comedy high as it gets, and it would have been enough. Then, in the third reel, he has to throw on drag. He joins an all-girl band to escape the wrath of Al Capone. And he does the travesty not only as well as it can be done but better than anyone has ever seen it. He plays a girl for keeps. He believes it, and we believe it. Then, dear reader, and I know you are nodding along with the report, he transforms himself into a millionaire in yachting costume and does the world's best imitation of Cary Grant.

This is a performance one wishes to hug to one's chest. It is the perfection of comic acting—idiosyncratic, loving, involved, and perfectly true.

Now we see him as *The Boston Strangler.* He plays Albert DeSalvo, the murderer. The camera follows him through various quite grisly stalkings and killings. We are shocked at the seeming reason of his motivation. These acts make perfect sense to the actor—and so we see not a monster but the human capacity (yours and mine) for monstrousness. Now DeSalvo is apprehended. A psychiatrist takes him through the crimes, of which, we discover, he was unaware. He does not remember them. And in the interrogation sessions we see DeSalvo, that is, Tony Curtis, recall, little by little, the grisly murders, and we see him, before our eyes, *disintegrate*.

These are some of the greatest moments of film acting.

We do not laud and revere Mr. Curtis's "great technique"; we merely remember the moments of his performance our entire lives.

Mike Nichols told me long ago that there is no such thing as a career—that if a person has done five great things over three decades of work she is indeed blessed. I will mention Mr. Curtis in *Sweet Smell of Success,* and as the escaping convict chained to Sidney Poitier in *The Defiant Ones,* and in *Trapeze,* and that is five. Let me also cite Robert Duvall in *Apocalypse Now,* who loved the smell of napalm in the morning; Frank Morgan, who asked Dorothy not to look behind the curtain in *The Wizard of Oz;* Hattie McDaniel in *Gone with the Wind,* who instructed us that "id just ain't fittin' "; Paul Muni, whose delivery of the tagline to *I Am a Fugitive from a Chain Gang* stopped hearts (Q. How do you live? A. I steal); Brando in *The Godfather;* Welles in *Citizen Kane;* Shelley Winters's dejection in *A Place in the Sun*. These are performances that make us smile sadly or grin. These are the work of *truly* great actors, great actors with a small *g,* of whom we remember, similarly, the noun and not the adjective.

GREAT AND ROTTEN ACTING

What an odd thing is preference. I have a preference for quiet.

There is a wonderful old weeper called *Penny Serenade* (1941). Here we have Irene Dunne and Cary Grant. Their little girl has died in the great Tokyo earthquake of nineteen twenty something, and they are, of course, bereft. They are awarded provisional custody of a young orphan and raise her for four years. Cary then loses his job—it is the Depression—and the orphanage informs him that he is therefore likely to lose custody of his daughter.

He goes to the judge and pleads. Now, *pleading* is, in my experience, the hardest thing for any actor to do. It involves, onstage or off, complete self-abasement, and (again, whether in life or onstage) it is *very* painful. Most actors, asked to plead, will counterfeit the act. This is called "indicating" and means creation of a recognizable rendition of the emotion supposedly required by the script.* Cary Grant, in a magnificent piece of acting, actually pleads. He bares his soul before the judge who holds the fate of his daughter in his hands.

The performance, however, that I count as ethereal, is the one occurring *behind* him. Beulah Bondi, playing the head of

---

* John Barrymore flinches to indicate surprise; Bela Lugosi narrows his eyes to indicate malevolence; Danny Kaye smiles to indicate charming harmlessness.

the orphanage, has, through the film, championed the cause of Cary and Irene. She has told them that the chances of the judge awarding the little girl to a family with no income are nil. She accompanies Cary to the chambers and sits, far off in the background, to watch the proceedings.

We know she is disposed toward the supplicant. We see that she has no wish to influence the judge. We *understand* that she feels that any emotion, utterance, any comment whatever would be detrimental to the case of the pleader and, *further,* that she believes in the system as constituted. She has intervened to what she considers the limit of the acceptable, and though it is painful, she will now withhold herself from the necessary operation of the court.

Beulah Bondi accomplishes all this through sitting and watching.

Or look at Celia Johnson in *In Which We Serve* (1942). She plays the wife of Captain Kinross (Noël Coward). In a party scene she toasts a young woman, newly betrothed to a naval officer. She recites the hardships the young woman has in store and concludes the toast in an encomium to the officer's ship. The speech, and its Ciceronian conclusion, are delivered completely without sentimentality. They are not emotionless; to the contrary, they are filled with the truth of emotion withheld.

In aid of what has the emotion been withheld? In favor of the truth.

Like Beulah Bondi, Celia Johnson will not sully the moment, she will not patronize the other player (nor, thus, the audience) with the *performance* of emotionality.

Look later in the film. Here is Noël Coward, as fine an actor as anyone could hope to see. As Captain Kinross he is bidding adieu to his shipmates. They have served together, been torpedoed together, spent days in the wreckage and in the boats of their ship, and now the company is being disbanded and dispersed.

They are in an empty warehouse. The company is at attention. He says, "Gather round," and the men all step in, and he speaks to them for a few moments. He tells them what an honor it has been to serve with them, that there is not one of them with whom he would not serve again, and then shakes their hands. The ship's company lines up, and Noël Coward says good-bye to each of the forty men. The camera is stationary, the line moves forward, and we see, in each of his farewells, the nature of his relationship with that man.*

See also Ward Bond in *Gentleman Jim* (1942). It's a boxing movie about Gentleman James J. Corbett (played by Errol Flynn) and his fight for the heavyweight title (1892) against the icon John L. Sullivan (played by Bond).

Flynn was, for my money, a great actor. It's easy to be taken in by his perfect looks, but film by film, scene by scene, he was always simple, always truthful, and always generous. Here, he's just conquered the unconquerable Sullivan and is making merry at the postfight bun-fight. But let's look at Bond. The room grows quiet as he enters. He walks up to Flynn and, in the most authentically humbled and humble performance, gives the new champ the title belt and wishes him well. (The scene is shot in two overs: over Bond onto Flynn, over Flynn onto Bond. But the performance is so simple and striking, the director and editor played the whole two-minute speech, unbroken, on Bond.)

I also recommend that you see Sidney Lumet's *Fail-Safe* (1964).

Henry Fonda is the president of the United States. Missiles have been sent in error against the Soviet Russians, and Fonda retires to a bomb shelter to speak on the hotline with the

* See also the congruent opening scene of *Dodsworth,* where Walter Huston, resigning from the automobile company he created twenty years ago, takes his leave, walking through the crowd of workers with whom he has built the company.

Soviet premier. Fonda is accompanied by his interpreter, played by Larry Hagman. The scene is just these two men in a bare white room. Hagman is talking to the Russians and translating for Fonda. The fate of the world depends on his translation. Fonda tells him to take it easy, listen carefully, take his time. He does. In this remarkable scene, it is nearly impossible to realize that they are but two actors in an imaginary situation in a set made of four white flats.

I am reminded of Ruth Draper.

For those unacquainted with her work, let me offer you a treat. Miss Draper wrote and performed one-woman dramas from the thirties through the fifties. Though they are monologues, it is insufficient, in fact, misleading, to identify them solely as such. They are true and complete dramas. She was, in my opinion, one of the great dramatists of the twentieth century.

One of her pieces is entitled "A Scottish Immigrant at Ellis Island." The group, of which she has been a part, is in line at Ellis Island, waiting for their interviews with American immigration. The young Scottish girl (played on the recording by Miss Draper, in her seventies) chats with the friends she has made. She goes on about her new life, the fiancé who is awaiting her, and she invites her friends to come visit them, after their marriage, in New Jersey. She exchanges about five lines with a young man. She tells him that she is very glad to have met him. To his reply (unheard by us), she responds that she will not forget him either, and she says good-bye.

We understand, in these five lines of hers, that the young man has fallen irrevocably in love with her and that he will for the rest of life regret their parting, that he may eventually marry, but he will never marry his love, the young girl he met on shipboard.

We further understand that the Scottish girl herself understands this but that she will not intrude; she will not sully the young man's good-bye with pity or sympathy; she will respond to his courage with courage.

All this in a few words spoken by an actress to a person who exists only in her imagination—and now in ours.

I recommend to you Roger Livesey in just about anything. He was, to me, the British Henry Fonda—the perfect actor, incapable of falsity. He and Anton Walbrook portray a British and a German officer from the Edwardian period through the Blitz. The film, *The Life and Death of Colonel Blimp* (1943) by Powell and Pressburger, is my favorite film. Livesey, as a young man, is dispatched on a diplomatic mission to Berlin. He insults a group of Junkers and must fight a duel. His opponent, appointed by the German army, is Walbrook. They meet for the first time in a dueling academy. As the Swedish judge instructs them in the code of the duel, they exchange looks with each other. We see that each assesses the other and, having found his opponent worthy—indeed, estimable—apologizes for the necessity of savagery and regrets that personal feelings must be subordinated to duty. All in two—silent—shots.

We all know what falsity looks like. How exhilarating to see truth.

GOOD IN THE ROOM:

AUDITIONS AND THE FALLACY OF TESTING

What makes some actors, some acting, and some performances false? Some of it is due to the character of the individual,
some to lack of commitment, or perhaps of talent, some to the
choices of the director, and much to the audition process.

I hate the audition process. Having experienced it as an
actor, I found it demeaning. As a writer and director, I find it
damn near useless.

The question, for the director, should not be "Can they act
the part?" but "Can they *act*?" The best way to determine the
applicant's skills is to watch his work.

If the applicant actually has something to offer—as evi-
denced in an actual performance—it should then be up to the
director to decide whether the actor's skills, personality, and
sensibilities make him a good choice for the particular part
being cast.

Why not just give him the script and "test" him on it (in
effect, the current system)? Well, because the ability to act is
not always paired with the ability to audition.

In the audition room, the actor is a supplicant. Othello
says, "Take me, take a soldier; take a soldier, take a King."
There we have not only the actor's fantasy but also his understanding of his life and his life's work: He is allowed, encouraged, and, if gifted, driven to cast himself in various enjoyable,

demanding roles and situations. These situations may not be noble, *but the work, and the joy of exploring them, is.*

The actor's ability to immerse himself freely, spontaneously, and generously is applauded, rightly, by the audience, who came to the play to be taken out of themselves. The more free the actor plays, the greater the enjoyment the audience derives.

But those across the table in the audition room are not an audience but a jury. They come not to a place of enjoyment but of drudgery.

Why? Because they spend the day disappointing people. It is taxing, constantly, to remember that though the mass of applicants is daunting, each individual is deserving of respect. The juror's attention may very well fray, and rather than indict himself, he may transfer his irritation to the next applicant. And the next. And the next. The actor, then, confronts not only a jury but also a short-tempered one.

The jurors gaze down what now seems to be a growing list of applicants and utter this prayer: "Let the next one be so bad that I may discard him immediately, thus reducing my burden." The process drags on. The jurors forget that they have come to make a discovery. They are no longer interested in discovery but in exclusion.

Why? Because *even discovery will not put a dent in their list.* The jurors are faced with an afternoon's attempt to cast one part, meaning even the joy occasioned (and that so rarely) by a brilliant performance will be immediately superseded by reserve and a return to somnolence. For the juror thinks (a) I still have twenty people to see, how could I *bear* those hours, knowing the part had already been cast?; thus, (b) I must *pace* myself. I loved this last actor, but perhaps I was deluded. Perhaps someone *even better* will come along.

And so the afternoon creeps on. Such that, at the end of the day, the initial reaction "this person is a *genius*" has been revised into "I remember I liked him very much. But was there not that *other* person, some hours later, who *also* had good qualities?"

(And it is not, I think, too Freudian to suggest that the brilliant auditioner *might* even create in the jurors some slight subconscious animosity—for was it not his audition that rendered the rest of the afternoon so problematical?)

Fatigued, angry, self-loathing (have they not heard hours of ungrantable petitions?), and confused, the jurors sit at the close of play. Each has dealt with the trauma/unpleasantness/waste/confusion differently. And this necessary difference in personality must and will manifest itself in differences of choice.

One committee member may have held out all afternoon for the brilliant actor; one, measuring not against the needs of the script but against this performance, may choose another. That is, having sat fuming for too many hours, this second juror may simply feel the need to exercise that autonomy denied him all day and strike out for the release occasioned by a true subjective choice, and let the demands of the play be damned. A third may find happiness in adopting the role of wise negotiator and counsel reserve: perhaps even *more* applicants should be seen, for if the appearance of even that one star was insufficient to create unanimity, would not wisdom suggest *something* in the fellow was somehow lacking?

The jurors have now fallen into a fatigue that they are happy to characterize as healthy caution. They no longer remember their original task, to find an actor who will enliven the part; they remember only that their brief is to "*cast* the part." They have long ceased being an audience—that is, a group that has come to be delighted. They would like to be a group of, if I may, serious, responsible judges, but they have no idea how such a group might operate.

Subjective opinion has been tried and called untrustworthy. Its day is past. What remains but consensus? Only consensus will get them out of the room. But consensus is, of course, the dead opposite of that subjectivity that is the essence of the theatrical experience.

The choice of a date, a mate, a home, a name for the baby are all transcendently subjective. Each is an assertion of an individual's understanding of his right to joy; none, finally, is capable of analysis. By each, the individual asserts that there is a mystery in life and that he is entitled to participate in it.

Consensus is all very well and good. It is the core of society: the commitment to a greater good than one's own instincts. No wonder the auditioning group defaults to it. (We may note that the group, here, has become like that small subsociety immediately formed by the twin extremities of shared hardship and isolation—e.g., the basic training platoon, the survivors of a shipwreck, et cetera. Here we may see the spontaneous appearance of the lawyer, the politician, the comedian, the peacemaker, the wise elder, the willing factotum, as each member stakes out his place in the new world, which, he sees, *demands* communal effort.)

The auditioning group, like the sequestered jury, which, in effect, it is, translates its concerns from *the originally stated task at hand* to *the welfare of the group*—i.e., "I was appointed to judge whether John Smith was guilty as charged. My task has *become* how to get myself and my group out of the jury room with some semblance of self-respect."

Psychologists Ernst Heinrich Weber and Gustav Theodor Fechner wrote on the abilities of the human mind to detect small changes: How small an alteration in musical tone, in the shade of a color, in the size of an object, et cetera, could the mind perceive? Would they had addressed, and so quantified, the capacity of the mind to retain and differentiate between a vast bunch of auditioners. One may perhaps (notes or no) retain the impressions of four to five, certainly not of twenty, as the auditioner discovers. And so, now firmly self-understood as *part of a jury,* he utters the phrase that is the foundation of society and the death of art: "What do *you* think?" Consensus, enshrined as right thinking, ensues, and the stage is set for mediocrity.

The first thing an actor does on achieving success is to stop auditioning. He broadcasts that phrase he has repressed, at some cost, during the years of his struggle: if they want to know what I do, let them view my work and then make up their *own* fool minds.

Yes, some actors audition well. Some have sufficient confidence or a sufficiently idiosyncratic makeup as to consider the audition, *in itself,* a performance (which is to say, potentially enjoyable). I have heard actors say so and been told that some soi-disant auditioning classes teach this viewing of the interview, and suggest that to accept this advice, to act upon it, would, and will, increase an actor's odds of employment. But what of the actor incapable of doing so? What of the actor who translates his affront at judgment into hatred of himself or the auditioners (such generally expressed as "nervousness")?

Well, this person is in a pickle. He is, in the cant of the trade, "not good in the room." His choices are limited to philosophy, self-help, and retreat. Many retire from the business, as they can't "get out of the room"; many resort to auditioning classes, hypnosis, mantras; and if they do not profit from these, many achieve that form of anesthesia known as "experience." Some reduce this "experience" into a set of axioms actually capable of bringing about the desired result: employment. Most fail.

And the folks on the hiring side of the table reason that the process, though harsh and though inexact, does possess the merit of winnowing out that which we, in our fatigue, may allow ourselves to think of as the weak. And yes, the show must go on, and Darwin, and so forth. But note that though occasionally a part may be cast quickly and, thus, in such a manner as to conduce to a continuance of such feelings in rehearsal and performance, the process in bulk is founded upon brutality.

See the actors auditioning for television. They read, first, for a casting agent. Normally these readings are put on tape and shown to producers and directors. Progression to the next step involves an in-person reading (of the same material from the script) with producers and directors. Those still surviving proceed to their presentation to the entity (usually a studio) funding the show. Lucky winners are now walked round to the network, the final hurdle between them and stardom.

Two, three, or four contestants for each part stand in the hall. Some go over their lines one, five, ten more last times; some perform relaxation exercises; some sit in a reverie or in contemplation. The scene resembles a locker room before a martial arts competition. Those who have trained together now perceive that their onetime comrades (those with whom they shared and share hardship, perception, and aspiration) are now their opponents. Each is alone and competes with all others for possession of that indivisible sum of success, wealth, approbation that is the part. One will prevail; the rest will be discarded.

But wait. Someone in authority is coming. How might he ameliorate this brutal situation? What does he hold in his hand?

These are contracts. For the applicants, had they misunderstood their position vis-à-vis the employer, must sign a contract *before* they are allowed into their final audition. That is, lest they consider themselves special (or, indeed, individual), they are reminded *by the force of law a contract holds* that they are replaceable, that they are interchangeable, and that they will not even get a *hearing* unless they so agree, legally and as the final act before they are ushered into the presence, that it is so.

The gladiators proclaimed before the contest, "We who are about to die salute you," thus perhaps invoking, and so perhaps participating in, the honor that, in spite of the horror, may exist in personal combat. But the actor proclaims, *legally,* that his pursuit of success, far from an example of honorable combat, is furthered only at the pleasure of an authority that subjugates all to money and that does not scruple to pit its employees against each other, financially, in a race to the bottom. (I do not know if this process of preemployment contract negotiation is legal. I suppose that it is legally defensible, which is saying little. And who among the aspiring actors would contest it? Such would, of course, be career-ending folly.)

Film—and to an exponentially greater degree, television—is just business. As film and television companies grow larger and more vertically integrated, they are ruled by businesspeople. Businesspeople are trained to quantify, and it, I am sure, makes good business sense to recast quondam aesthetical decisions as cost vs. benefit. But the bottom line, in art, in entertainment, and even in the entertainment industry, is the pleasure of the audience.

This pleasure *cannot* be quantified. It may be propitiated *only* by schooled, but *equally subjective,* decisions on the part of the artist.

Businesspeople have always resisted not only such decisions *but also the notion that such productive subjectivity exists.* Their inclination and training rejects it, and they recur in its supposed nonexistence not to the quantifiable (the audience's whim may not be quantified) but to the *imaginable.* That is, as they have experienced the benefits of consensus (in a committee meeting, it gets people out of the room; in a consumerate, it brings money to the purveyor), they seek to apply it, inductively and deductively, and at all times.

"See," they say, "though we thought ourselves faced with a situation that seemed to admit of neither solution nor grounds for arriving at same (casting), we have made a choice!" and, "As this magic of consensus worked in the room, must we not further reason that it will work in the auditorium? Let us, therefore, *imagine* that the audience arrives at decisions much as we do here: in committee."

Entertainment businesspeople worship this supposed tool of consensus. As well they should, for it is the only tool they have. They are lost in the wilderness and prefer, as might you or I, a broken compass to no compass at all.

They take this tool to the public in test screenings and focus groups. Here the audience is invited to replace its capacity for amusement with the right of sitting in judgment.*

These invited test screeners *never engage* that portion of

---

* Studio folks famously opine that testing is "just another tool" and that it would be foolish to overlook the use of any tool. This might seem, at first glance, simple common sense. But consider: When choosing an accountant it might make sense to take into account his or her age and, thus, expected working lifespan. Now, there is a medically proven correlation between longevity and percentage of body fat. Why not, then, test potential accountants for body fat to predict their potential working lifespan—why reject that tool? Because in utilizing it, one might weed from the applicant pool accountants of greater skill but higher body fat. Though there may be a correlation between body fat and expected working lifespan, there is none between body fat and skill in accountancy; thus, the utilization of this "tool," far from being helpful, is actually destructive. Similarly, while it might seem "common sense" to quiz viewers on their reactions to a film, there is *no correlation between these test results and a film's performance.* Thus, attention to these tests must and does mitigate against the release of films which, although they do not "test" well, might actually *perform* better than their more sanctioned brethren.

the human mind that loves a story; no, they have become enmeshed in a fantasy of business, and they now work to imagine (as did those folks in the committee/audition room) what some notional *other* group might just like. And they vote accordingly, thumbs-up, thumbs-down, in self-congratulation at having suspended that obviously now puerile, wide-eyed state of enjoyment of the unlicensed, unschooled, and mere "member of the audience."

This extended fallacy of consensus accounts, if not for the worthlessness, at least for the uniformity of most mass entertainment. For each human being is different. And the idiosyncrasy of the artist, this supposedly (by the executive) *divisive* tropism, is actually an ability to compel—to compel a disparate group of people not into a jury capable of consensus but into a group willing to suspend its rational capacity—into an *audience*.

We may note further that the executive, in forming a lay and random group into a committee supposedly capable of forecasting dramatic success, indicts, and in fact *unsays,* his protestation of his own possession of superior financial or mercantile powers. For if a regular person wandering in a mall somewhere may be shanghaied into watching a test screening, and if his opinion, and the opinions of his like, are the basis upon which executives determine how to place their bets, why not eliminate the executives entirely and proceed directly to the mall wanderer? Which is effectively what has happened in the casting session.

CRITICS

It is a comfort to ascribe to the process of film criticism, if not *justice,* then at least a certain symmetry.

"Well," we beleaguered say, "they shat on my beautiful work *this* time, but, sigh, last time they praised certain aspects of the film I thought I might have done better"; or, truth be told, "they trashed my film, but at least the swine also trashed the film of a hated competitor."

One reads mindless, hurried, self-serving dissections of the films of others, if not with glee, then with a certain praiseworthy equanimity; such holding of one's own feet to the fire, however, prompts a recourse to the philosophic. "Who *are* these brigands?" one wonders. "And who died and left them boss?" This, in the sufficiently irate, leads to fantasies not of outright crime but of *un revers de satire.*

One imagines the critic (in general perceived as, if not actually possessing, a second-rate intellect) in debate with the more mentally nimble filmmaker. One fantasizes about the critic himself taking to art and hazarding his good name "on his own bottom," et cetera. One may, in an extended violent reverie, wake to shame and find one's thought driven ever eastward, toward the stoicism of the Mediterranean and, in absolute extremis, toward the quest for satori of Nepal.

For critics are a plague.

Being of an especially weak nature, I find my bellicosity easily awakened in the face of injustice (to myself). Injustice in the lack of preparation, appreciation, and intelligence by the critics, or, indeed, injustice in the very fact of my being criticized. I do not think I am alone.

As ants at a picnic, however, the critics will not go away, and as I (qua writer and director) do not plan to go away, I have had to learn to deal with them.

The only effective method I have found, unfortunately, is to ignore them.

Artists loathe critics, and critics know it, and artists know they know it and know that the critics view and must view any attempt at rapprochement as meeching.

Any artist of any worth is absolutely his or her own harshest critic, and a critic's gracious studied ignorance of an artistic solecism is more likely to bring about its correction than would a snide riposte.

What of trash? Is it not the critic's job to cleanse it from the public view? No.

The critic's job in America is to sell newspapers. Newspapers are sold by gossip, and most critics write gossip—they invite the reader to find fault, licensing a vicarious superciliousness.

This practice increases not only readership but also, more importantly, advertising revenues, as the more films come and go, the more films have to pour out an initial rollout ad campaign. One is as unlikely to find a champion of the public taste in the arts section as to find a champion of actual defense in the Defense Department.

The officials of that department exist to defend their department, as do the officials of the arts section. Such are effectively not critics but censors, hired to defend the status quo.

Like censors, they may perhaps be bribed.

Spend enough money on a film and enough money on its ad campaign, and the newspaper *will* absolutely respond, if not with a guaranteed good review, then with sufficient on-and-off-the-page coverage to approximate such a review's result—an increased opening-week turnout.

Is there such a thing as a good critic? Yes. I think my work has benefited over the years from one or two such. Were such supporters of my work? Yes.

But, in the main, I don't like critics, and I like even less my personal inability to come to peace with the phenomenon. I might cite my benefits derived from certain critics and name them—but would it be possible to name them without the wish that they might read, and I might, thus, not only propitiate them but have wished to do so as well? It is a philosophic can of worms, indeed, it is.

And what of the "democratization of criticism," e.g., online critics? Well, this approaches pure gossip, and, as such, it is of necessity messier and more truthful than its licensed brother. In the end, we all have to take our knocks.

THE CRITIC AND THE CENSOR

Who are those people by whom you wish to be admired? Are they not these about whom you are in the habit of saying they are mad?

What, then? Do you wish to be admired by the mad?

—Epictetus*

Mr. Kipling wrote, "Tho' he who held the longer purse might hold the longer life." Similarly, the leniency of the critics of our great newspapers is proportional to the advertising budget of the offender. And who would have it otherwise? In days of yore, and still into our day, the former gossip columnist or sports reporter, and the otherwise unassignable, along with

---

* A long contemplation of this stoical view has left me but little better equipped to deal with the scorn of those I consider the untutored. But, recently, I have found that an increase (marginal but real) in my practicable stoicism by reasoning thus: We, (the artist), traditionally characterize our detractors as fools; therefore, to wish their good opinion is inconsistent. They (as you or I) may or may not be fools; they are, however, incontrovertibly, merchants of derision. Bad reviews sell. But, as the critic must occasionally praise (if only to preserve the illusion of open-mindedness), and if this praise—as it seems to be—is awarded *arbitrarily,* then, to wish for the critics' praise is *to wish that his censure fall on another.* Thus, to wish for critical praise is not merely inconsistent, but immoral, as it is a wish for another's suffering. Will time prove that I have allowed this progressed understanding to increase my peace of mind, and, thus, my utility to the body politic? I doubt it.

the (misguided) seeker after distinction, found, in practice, that their sway as critics had upon it the check of a rational concern, on the part of their employers, for the bottom line. The critical system may reek, to the politically savvy, of the old-fashioned retail depredations of the ward heeler—the mere settling of grudges or the promotion of some pet theory, grudge, or paramour that has traditionally been the recompense for the critic's poor pay and boring evenings.

It can be noted that advertisers, that is, those with money to burn, would, being human, expect a little warmth in return for providing the conflagration. That warmth was and is understood to be, to put it genteelly, "the benefit of the doubt." As it has been said, "Who would want to live in a town where you can't fix a parking ticket?"

Laws of eminent domain have been used for centuries to allow the state to condemn the property of the individual so that it may be used to benefit many (e.g., for the building of a dam, a road, a school). Recently, jurists have expanded the theory to allow the condemnation of any property, domestic or otherwise, that is not, in their view, generating sufficient tax revenue.

We may thank the Lord that, as we imagine and must pray is the case, a cast-iron conscience in some members of these committees of condemnation has resisted what must have been the strong, many, and varied inducements offered by the interested to misuse their wide-ranging powers.

But imagine the corruption inherent in an unchecked power to condemn. Might not the individual property holder, pitted against the power of the state and that power ceded, or cedable, to the highest bidder, not tremble and not inquire what he, in his powerlessness, might do to avert catastrophe? And might not a writer, painter, filmmaker, dramatist, or choreographer, faced with the threat of state-sanctioned censure, school himself early on to think twice?

The sobering specter of purity-of-speech and purity-of-image laws should concern all artists. In such a day, may God forbid it, our job will be done; the critic no longer will even be persuadable, and we may well yearn for that innocent day.

CRIMES AND MISDEMEANORS

MANNERS IN HOLLYWOOD

> They who lack talent expect things to happen without effort.
> —Eric Hoffer

Were we to construe manners in the contemporary sense of *bienséance,* this chapter would be rather short, as such manners do not exist in Hollywood. Considered, as *moeurs,* however, a survey of Hollywood manners might offer an afternoon of happy occupation to the strong-stomached anthropologist.

The adage "Don't look at the downed man" applies equally in combat and in the trenches of film production.

The observed rule in Hollywood is: "Feel free to treat everyone like scum, for if they desire something from you, they'll just have to put up with it, and should they rise to wealth and power, any past civility shown toward them will either be forgotten or remembered as some aberrant and contemptible display of weakness."

I shall not overtax the reader's credulity with tales of film-world savagery, for such tales must impose upon either his belief or his sense of outrage.

"What?" the affronted might say. "I bought (or—may heaven forfend—borrowed) this book for entertainment, and I am asked to debase myself in attention to an unclean recital."

Well, then, may my recital (for I cannot remain continent) be entertaining.

Among my favorites is the director, flown with his wife and family on the studio jet to Hawaii, for his film's opening.

It bombed, and on application to the airport, the director was told the jet had left. He intuited this to mean that he and his family were free to find their own way back home.

This is the template for the difficult passage in Hollywood—the offending party becomes not merely persona non grata but dead. I do a film with a longtime colleague, a producer. He makes a deal with the Eurotrash money folk to sell the film out. He forms a corporate partnership with them and, halfway through the film, refuses to take my calls and those of the editorial department, whose cash has been cut off and who cannot buy supplies. I finally get him on the phone. "I'm sick of carrying water for you people," he says. A relationship of twenty years.

Before the relationship (inevitably) goes wrong, all is toast and jam—sweet but bloating; after the first contretemps, war to the knife.

The exception: that interchange wherein the parties' relative status is unclear. This awakens, in those who sit on the other side of the table, apprehension, and so its expression as anger, masked as awkwardness. The technical term for the above is, I believe, smarminess (e.g., "I'm a great fan of yours. Great, great, very great"). The newcomer to Hollywood must feel like a high-functioning autistic, forced to resort to mnemonics and cheat sheets to remember how to behave in the most simple situations.

A sample list:

Should the project go awry, you will be notified by a complete lack of contact with those in whose hands its administration has rested.

Attempts to contact them will be met by the response that "she is in conference," "on vacation," or, my favorite, "out of town"—as if film executives spent any waking moment, in whatever part of the globe, other than on the phone and constantly connected to their office.

Like that autistic, the response, "Well, she may be out of town, but surely she calls in for messages; please have her return my call" is discovered by the neophyte to be other than the thing. Silence greeting such a commonplace observation is like that vouchsafed the five-year-old at the dinner party who announces that his parents have oral sex.

Any bad news expressed, rather than left to the imagination of the offending, is delivered by the lowest-possible ranked henchperson, each placeholder above that nadir understanding the essential law of the new Medes and Persians: "I need not perform any act not immediately fungible." Manners in Hollywood, in short, stink on ice.

The Academy of Motion Picture Arts and Sciences issues, each year, the Jean Hersholt Humanitarian Award.

Jean Hersholt was a character actor in the thirties and forties, and one may note that he is remembered only as a nonentity and a nice guy, and one may draw his own conclusions.

Nelson said, "Aft the most honor, forward the better man." And I agree.

The working people in Hollywood (if you have not, by this point in the book, divined my prejudices) are the salt of the earth. The motion picture industry has repaid their devotion by moving most film production out of the country. Toronto, Montreal, Belgrade, and *London* are being shot for New York.

Any business is, if not essentially, at least potentially, pillage. The surest sign of voracity and corruption is the formation of "industry standards"—a collusion of capital to muscle labor and bilk the consumer (cf. the Hayes office, the Motion Picture Academy, those opposed to Janet Jackson's breast). The desire to cover the legitimate, messy operations of commerce with a mask of sanctity reveals what the cops call "guilty knowledge"—that is, that someone is getting screwed.

Robert Evans wrote in his book *The Kid Stays in the Picture* that the best films seem to come from the most troubled sets, but with respect to Mr. Evans, I think this is a bunch of hogwash. I think that a *producer* likes a troubled set, because it allows him to "save the day" and otherwise exert undue and unfortunate influence upon a mechanism that, had he been doing his job correctly, should have run smoothly in the first place.

Were I king, I would make all the youth fomenting in film schools study deportment; for the good producer, director, agent, manager might then couple, or indeed promote, self-interest by civility—as does a *truly* smart businessperson, advancing, as has been said, to his own goals by taking the other fellow's road.

For to live in an uncivil world is debasing. It, of course, corrupts the practitioner, and it demoralizes those practiced upon, offering them the choice of learning either character or servility, and so perhaps my argument is warped, and in the stringency of life in a boorish land, there might be found some possibility of good.

But in the words of Bosquet, "C'est magnifique, mais ce n'est pas la guerre."

THEFT

Everybody on the production end always assumes the writer is stealing their money.

On the writer's side of the table, everybody always assumes the unit production manager (the comptroller) is stealing, and everybody *knows* the producer is stealing, and the thefts of the distributor are a certainty surpassing the necessity of discussion.

But among the dramatic arts and crafts, only the writer, I believe, is assumed to be criminal.

One would not accuse an actor or director of malingering—their obvious self-interest in a merchantable product bearing their name would render absurd accusations of less-than-best effort, but almost all writing for hire I have done, and almost all of that done by my colleagues, has ended with these accusations by the producers or studios: you did not do enough, you did not do as you were asked, you spent too little time, et cetera.

This is coupled to a disposition on the part of the employer to accept *nothing* as a completed job. The writer contractually obligates himself to do a certain number of revisions. These are called, variously, "drafts," "sets" (of revisions), and "polishes" and are known collectively as "steps." However many steps the writer has signed on for—that is, however many times he has agreed, contractually, to accept corrections and implement them—someone on the other side of the table *will* either request or demand more work. This demand takes two major forms: the request, "I know what we both agreed to, but would you mind, as a favor . . . ," and its corollary, "I know what we agreed to, but refusal would be endangering not only the project but your reputation; why would you want to shoot yourself in the foot—aren't you a team player?"

The more minatory form is an outright or implied accusation of fraud: "You have not done as asked, you sloughed it off, you intend to defraud me. . . ."

O, poor writer. For I do not find the writer any less agreeable to concerted effort than the actor, director, or designer. Yet, the thing, for the writer, usually ends in recriminations.

I know there are those homeowners who always end by suing their contractors or decorators, and those decorators, et cetera, who end every contract in court. And so it is with the writer.

His urge to see the thing through, to be agreeable, to do a good job, to be well thought of, to protect his reputation in the mercantile community is accompanied by the unpleasant certainty that *someone* will most likely finally turn combative.

In addition to the usual human desire for peace, the writer dreads the havoc that continued extracontractual and, indeed, extrarational work will produce on his script.

For any project, whether the screenplay for an epic or your wife's hairdo, can be ruined by too much freely given advice, and no advice is given more freely than that supposedly correcting the fool errors of the screenwriter.

The problem is further worsened by its (to the writer) interminability. Once he gives in to cajolement or threat, he may assume such will be continued, for he is, in accepting unmannerly (as extracontractual) corrections, encouraging their continuation. (By agreeing to agree to do more than that to which he, contractually, agreed, the writer confirms in the producer, studio head, et cetera, the truth of their original prejudice: that the writer, in effect, *is* no good, and that all his work is approximate, and its worth arguable at best.)

If one treated an architect thusly ("Would you mind moving the staircase? Thank you. Now would you mind moving the skylight?"), one would quickly come to find in his acquiescence disturbing evidence of the architect's lack of structural understanding.

So does the noodger come, by the process of his cajolement, to ratify an incipient prejudice: that the writer has no damn idea what he is talking about and that the previously undiscovered literary powers of the employer had best come to the fore fast and clean house.

In the script, change follows change until, inevitably, the producer comes to the inescapable conclusion that the writer, and his now indecipherable pile of shit, must be thrown out and a new broom must sweep clean. The concern—"How can I be sure you're not going to rob me?"—is revealed as prescient when the nervous producer finds himself left with the mud he and his colleagues' notes have wrought.

No wonder all writers want to direct: one still has to put up with a load of nonsense, but even if wearing two hats (writer and director), there is one under which one is not called a thief and then raped.

TWO GREAT AMERICAN DOCUMENTS; OR,
IN THE WAKE OF THE OSCARS

In a document that purports to be the Antioch College Sexual Offense Prevention Policy (SOPP) (1994):

> The spirit of Antioch's Sexual Prevention Policy is about 'yes' . . . The spirit is about a fully affirmative YES. Not an ambiguous yes, or a well-not-really-but-ok-I-guess yes . . . This is about YES, UM HUM, ABSOLUTELY YAHOO YES! . . . Being with someone you are sure YOU REALLY WANT to be with THAT is EXCITING, is EROTIC, is DEEP, is GREAT, is YES! That is consent. That is the spirit of the policy.

It is exhilarating to be part of a community that is working so hard to increase equality and mutual satisfaction and to rectify domination and oppression.

And from the Academy of Motion Picture Arts and Sciences 2003 pamphlet on Academy Standards:

> There are many within the Academy today . . . who use the phrase "Academy campaign" without irony or embarrassment. It is not at all necessary, though, that such a concept or such a thing exist.
>
> The simplest most direct path to protecting the Academy Awards Process from debasement real or suspected would

be to arrive at a point at which electioneering disappeared entirely.

I envision, thus, a perfect world in which both the randy young at Antioch and the careerist film producer find a playing field as level as that which God intended.

In this world the lion shall lie down with that lamb, and only with that lamb that has spelled out its consent, vide Antioch:

> If the level of sexual intimacy increases . . . (i.e., if two people move from kissing while fully clothed . . . to undressing for direct physical contact, which is another level), the people involved need to express their clear verbal consent before moving to that new level.

But how, in what is clearly the heat of the moment, will they remember to turn aside and consider, so as to fulfill both the letter and the spirit of the law?

Our other document may help.

> The Academy does not presume to tell its members when they may and may not invite friends to their homes . . . at the same time, the Oscar-season "parties" that in fact are heavy-handed lobbying occasions have become . . . distasteful. . . . Self-tests for whether a dinner party really is a dinner or a party, as distinct from a tactical maneuver in an Oscar campaign, include the following . . .

Which list is an aide for (and a caution to) those ethically conflicted about the true nature of their canapés.

The Academy, much like the stoics of an earlier day, suggests the conflicted consider his motives and, if still in doubt, review who is footing the bill for the entertainment. Is it the host himself or a studio or production company? Are guests invited in the hope that they have gained an appreciation of the artist and his difficulties "faced and overcome" during filming?

" 'Yes' answers indicate treacherous ethical waters."

These clarifying documents, in common with *The Rights of Man,* et cetera, exist to force one's attention to abuses to which the perpetrator or victim has become desensitized. The first step toward a recompleted humanity, then, must necessarily be shock at the gulf between our practice and right reason; e.g., "All sexual contact and conduct between any two (or more!) people must be consensual."

But there will always be collusion. Collusion is, indeed, the true and necessary state of communal endeavor. Just as it seems that money is to be made in the stock market *only* by what the deluded know by the sobriquet "insider trading," so, according to the solons of Antioch, healthy sex can be ensured among the young only by a watchfulness as that of our friends the Medes and the Persians.

For will not the young collude and conspire against law, reason, custom, and tradition in order to hide the salami? And will not the depraved fame- and fortune-starved members of the Academy serve ceviche in an other-than-disinterested manner?

In short, yes.

To speak of the movie business, which is my assigned beat: wherever there is community secrecy and the possibility of invidious gain, there must be collusion.

The human mind cannot tolerate the spectre of waste presented by the possibility of chicanery without detection. The very vehemence with which the Academy presents its good-willed and patient plea informs as to the impossibility of its implementation.

For, in each, the fault is not with the participants but with their stars.

The young will not stop copulating like rabbits, and no amount of what is, finally, voyeurism and child abuse on the part of the school administration will turn them from the course of lust. Neither will the members of AMPAS cease voting for their self-interest, which is, and must be, the nature of all awards ceremonies.

The movies are a cutthroat business, the business is entertainment, and we should be glad of the entertainment value of a bunch of pirates proclaiming their mutual goodwill and probity.

Perhaps even extending to ourselves the same licensed smirk of the randy Antioch elders and receiving the same necessary rejoinder: "Okay. You first."

CONCLUSION:
IT AIN'T OVER TILL IT'S OVER

Stanislavsky wrote that the last ninety seconds are the most important in the play. Hollywood wisdom casts it thus: Turn the thing around in the last two minutes, and you can live quite nicely. Turn it around again in the last ten seconds and you can buy a house in Bel Air.

This is old-style moviemaking, wherein the loveless child relents, the previously suspect suitor is found to be "good" and gets the girl, and the wandering minstrel is revealed as the king.

We have, also, the surprise/shock ending, e.g., *Diabolique, Witness for the Prosecution, The Sixth Sense.* He who could fool the canny moviegoer up to the last beat *should* have a house in Bel Air, or whatever else his heart desires. Does he not deserve it? Absolutely. For movies do not exist to make us better but to give us a thrill or chill on Wednesday night when we are out with our best gal.

If the shark makes us say "ooh," it has earned our few dollars. If the filmmaker can make us say "ooh" of a shot of the empty water, give him his private plane.

"There are three degrees of bliss," Mr. Kipling instructed us, "at the foot of Allah's throne/and the lowest place is his/who has saved a soul by a jest."

I offer the punch line of *Some Like It Hot* as good a way of getting offstage as one could wish:

Jack Lemmon: "I'm a man."

Joe E. Brown: "Well, nobody's perfect."

What are the great endings of art? "Reader, I married him," and "Ol' Man River, he jes keeps rollin' along." Equaled in the cinema, perhaps, by the shock/surprise endings listed above and "The sonofabitch stole my watch" from *The Front Page* and Paul Muni's tag from *I Am a Fugitive from a Chain Gang:* Q: "How do you live?" Muni's answer: "I steal."

In contrast to the perfectly acceptable "I'll never leave Kansas again" or "Tomorrow is another day," there are endings that introduce new, and transformative, information in the last seconds of the film.

The Pride of the Yankees is a rather good baseball biography. Gary Cooper, playing Lou Gehrig, the world's greatest player, is dying of a wasting disease. He is given a farewell party by his New York Yankees at Yankee Stadium. He is honored, and cheered, and declares himself "the luckiest man who ever lived." He then hobbles off the field, supported by his beloved wife, Teresa Wright, walking into a medium long shot, stadium corridor, day. And as he walks from us, as we begin to stir, knowing the movie over, we hear the umpire in the distance shouting, "Play *ball*."

This, to me, is great filmmaking. The information introduced is new and inevitable-familiar: the filmmakers have apostrophized their potentially sententious tribute (both the stadium fete and the film) in the name of a greater ideal: the game goes on.

Sailor of the King is a World War I–World War II tale. Michael Rennie is a British naval officer. In Canada, during the first war, he meets a young woman, they become intimate, but before they can marry, Michael is called away, then peace breaks out.

One war later, he is again in command at sea. A young ensign, Jeffrey Hunter, is taught the ways of command and taken under Rennie's wing, and Rennie treats him as the son he never had. Near the end of the film they lay up in a Canadian port, and Jeffrey Hunter confesses that he himself is Canadian and, perhaps, while they are at port, Rennie would like to meet his mother. We understand that the mother will be revealed to Rennie as his inamorata of the first war—the punch line of the whole thing is that Jeffrey Hunter is in truth his son.

This, while not illuminating, is enjoyable, and what is wrong with that?

On the other hand, *Cocoon* is a pretty good film. All the old folk go up in the sky at the end. And then we gather around the grave site of Hume Cronyn, who, as I remember, didn't quite have the bottle for the trip. The fellow playing the pastor does the eulogy well and then says, "Let us pray"; we see him lift his eyes skyward. I saw it and thought: *This,* now, is bold filmmaking. It is as completive as the final chord of *Tristan* and lacks only the funny hats.

Yes. *Cocoon* is not a story about space critters come down to Earth but about old people learning to face death. It is a spiritual journey. Yes, let us pray that when our time comes we can face the end with perhaps the same good humor and philosophy that the filmmakers face at the end of *their* journey.

And then the thing went on one beat too long. We were transported from the graveside to a spaceship, where we again saw Don Ameche et al., and I found, to my chagrin, that the film, no, was in fact about space critters.

"I love you" does pretty well as the end of a speech. It generally is not advisable to follow it by "and one more thing. . . ."

We remember "Au revoir, sale Juif" at the end of *Grand Illusion,* Jean Gabin's ironic farewell to his comrade, Dalio.

And Warner Baxter sitting alone by the stagedoor fire escape at the conclusion of *42nd Street,* sitting alone and unremarked as the hit play's adoring fans praise all contributions but his own.

How might one achieve this perfect completion?

First, the problem of the play must be concise. Then, the progress toward it must be direct and all incidents essential either in advancement or disruption of that progress. Finally, the conclusion must be definite (e.g., France is freed, the couple is reunited, the treasure is returned to its rightful owner).

These three steps are difficult to accomplish. The play is a syllogism, and to function perfectly, it must be structured perfectly. If A, then B.

It can take place on any level of abstraction: In order to save France, I must discover how to land on the beaches. In order to land on the beaches, I must produce a small craft cheaply and in vast numbers; in order to do so, I must obtain an enormous amount of cypress; in order to do so, I must win the trust of the crotchety octogenarian who holds the deed to . . . , et cetera.

So, my efforts to obtain that one piece of silverware that would convince the octogenarian to deed me the cypress that would allow me to build the boats. These efforts are essential to allow me to save France—each small step is essential to the clearly formulated superobjective, and the audience will follow the story, wondering what happens next.

Q. Is it possible to engross the audience when the end of the quest is already known?

Yes. Mark Twain wrote of U. S. Grant's personal memoirs that they were so well written as to make one wonder who was going to win the Civil War.

It is *more difficult* to engross the audience in a biography, as the end is known. It calls for greater skill and imagination on the part of the writer in finding an *internal* story within the generally known historical moment.

This story is usually boy-meets-loses-gets-girl. In my previous example—the quest for a piece of silverware—the idea is the same.

The superobjective may, indeed, be *concealed* from the audience. If the progress of the incidents—war, amphibious assault boats, cypress, old lady, silverware—is direct and essential, it could, indeed, be inverted, so that what seems to be a movie about matching flatware turns out to be about saving Western civilization.

Here the audience, if sufficiently engrossed, again, scene to scene, is rewarded in the last ten seconds by the revelatory recasting of the goal. They discover, in *The Sixth Sense,* that they have not been watching Bruce Willis's compassionate efforts to help a disturbed youngster with his clairvoyance but, rather, watching the youngster help Bruce come to terms with his own death.

In *Pygmalion* we are told—and find, of course—that we *knew* Eliza Doolittle was "going to marry Freddy." And in *The Pride of the Yankees* we are put in the same position as Lou Gehrig and discover that baseball itself is deeper in our hearts than our love even of its most perfect avatar.

God bless the writer who can do this, and let him or her retire, with our blessings, to the pleasures of Bel Air, whatever they may be.

Play ball.

APPENDIX:
FILMS REFERENCED

The Adventures of Baron Munchausen (1988)
Starring: John Neville, Eric Idle, Sarah Polley. Director: Terry Gilliam. Written by Charles McKeown and Terry Gilliam; 126 minutes; Allied Filmmakers. Traveling with a group of misfits, a seventeenth-century aristocrat has some truly unbelievable experiences throughout Europe.

An American Tragedy (1931)
Starring: Phillips Holmes, Sylvia Sidney, Frances Dee. Director: Josef von Sternberg. Written by Samuel Hoffenstein, adapted from the classic novel by Theodore Dreiser; 96 minutes; Paramount Pictures. A working-class man finds himself torn between his love for a rich woman and his love for a lower-class coworker.

Angels in America (2003)
Starring: Al Pacino, Meryl Streep, Emma Thompson. Director: Mike Nichols. Written by Tony Kushner; 352 minutes; Avenue Pictures Productions. Miniseries based on Tony Kushner's play series about the American AIDS epidemic during the 1980s and its effects on a closeted Mormon man, a gay couple, and the notoriously homophobic lawyer Roy Cohn.

Apocalypse Now (1979)
Starring: Marlon Brando, Martin Sheen, Robert Duvall. Director: Francis Ford Coppola. Written by John Milius, Francis Ford Coppola, and Michael Herr; 153 minutes; Zoetrope Studios. An adaptation of the classic Conrad novella *Heart of Darkness*, set in the Vietnam War, in which an Army captain goes on a dangerous mission to dethrone Kurtz, a Green Beret who has gone mad.

Arsenic and Old Lace (1944)

Starring: Cary Grant, Josephine Hull. Director: Frank Capra. Written by Julius J. and Philip G. Epstein, adapted from the play by Joseph Kesserling; 118 minutes; Warner Brothers. A young man discovers that insanity runs in his family and that his two aunts have been poisoning lonely old men and hiding their bodies in the basement.

Back to Bataan (1945)

Starring: John Wayne, Anthony Quinn. Director: Edward Dymtryk. Written by Ben Barzman and Richard H. Landau, based on the story by William Gorden and Æneas Mackenzie; 95 minutes; RKO Radio Pictures. After the Philippines fall to the Japanese in World War II, a rogue American army colonel stays behind and organizes an underground resistance movement to oppose the occupation.

Bambi Meets Godzilla (1969)

Director: Marv Newland. Written by Marv Newland; 2 minutes; Rhino Wea. In this animated short, the sympathetic deer, Bambi, meets the ultimate monster, Godzilla.

Battleship Potemkin (1925)

Starring: Aleksandr Antonov, Vladimir Barsky. Director: Sergei M. Eisenstein. Written by Sergei M. Eisenstein and Nina Agadzhanova; 75 minutes; Goskino. Classic silent film about a violent mutiny on board a Russian battleship that leads to an uprising and, later, a massacre in Odessa.

Ben-Hur (1959)

Starring: Charlton Heston, Jack Hawkins. Director: William Wyler. Written by Karl Tunberg, adapted from the novel by General Lew Wallace; 212 minutes; Metro-Goldwyn-Mayer. A Jewish prince is forced into slavery after being betrayed by a lifelong Roman friend; after his release, he seeks his revenge.

The Birth of a Nation (1915)

Starring: Lillian Gish, Mae Marsh, Henry B. Walthall. Director: D. W. Griffith. Written by Frank E. Woods, Thomas F. Dixon Jr., and D. W. Griffith; 187 minutes; David W. Griffith Corp. This silent classic looks at the aftermath of the Civil War in a deeply racist light and glorifies the Ku Klux Klan.

The Bishop's Wife (1947)

Starring: Cary Grant, Loretta Young, David Niven. Director: Henry Koster. Written by Leonardo Bercovici and Robert E. Sherwood, adapted from the book by Robert Nathan; 109 minutes; Samuel Goldwyn Company. While having difficulties executing plans to have a cathedral built, a bishop prays for help and receives counsel from an angel, but the angel advises him about a completely different problem.

The Blair Witch Project (1999)

Starring: Heather Donahue, Joshua Leonard, Michael Williams. Director: Daniel Myrick and Eduardo Sanchez. Written by Daniel Myrick and Eduardo Sanchez; 86 minutes; Haxan Films. While making a documentary in the woods, three students disappear. A year later their haunting footage is seen for the first time.

The Blue Lamp (1950)

Starring: Jack Warner, Jimmy Hanley, Dirk Bogarde. Director: Basil Dearden. Written by T.E.B. Clarke; 84 minutes; Ealing Studios. As two cops go about their day, they find it interrupted by the discovery of a grisly murder of a fellow officer.

Bob le Flambeur (1955)

Starring: Isabelle Corey, Daniel Cauchy, Roger Duchesne. Director: Jean-Pierre Melville. Written by Auguste Le Breton and Jean-Pierre Melville; 98 minutes; Organisation Générale Cinématographique. A kindly down-on-his-luck gambler decides to stage a casino robbery with a pair of street kids and steal $800 million.

Bombardier (1943)

Starring: Brigadier General Eugene L. Eubank, Pat O'Brien, Randolph Scott. Director: Richard Wallace. Written by John Twist and Martin Rackin; 99 minutes; RKO Radio Pictures. A fast-moving documentary chronicling the lives and training of World War II bombers.

The Boston Strangler (1968)

Starring: Tony Curtis, Henry Fonda, George Kennedy. Director: Richard Fleischer. Written by Edward Anhalt, adapted from the book by Gerold Frank; 116 minutes; Twentieth Century Fox. During the 1960s, the Boston Strangler terrorized women, killing old, lonely women and tying pantyhose around their necks. This film re-creates the events that led to his capture.

The Bourne Identity (2002)

Starring: Matt Damon, Franka Potente, Chris Cooper. Director: Doug Liman. Written by Tony Gilroy and W. Blake Herron, adapted from the novel by Robert Ludlum; 119 minutes; The Kennedy/Marshall Company. Jason Bourne has no memory of who he is, what he does, or where he is from. All he knows is that he speaks several languages, knows how to fight, and that lots of people want him dead.

Brief Encounter (1945)

Starring: Celia Johnson, Trevor Howard. Director: David Lean. Written by Noel Coward; 86 minutes; Cineguild. Two married strangers begin an intense love affair after a chance encounter at a train station, meeting every Thursday in an attempt to sustain their passion.

Bullitt (1968)

Starring: Steve McQueen, Robert Vaughn, Jacqueline Bisset. Director: Peter Yates. Written by Alan Trustman and Harry Kleiner, adapted from the novel by Robert L. Fish; 113 minutes; Solar Productions. After a federal witness is killed, a tough cop seeks the victim's murderer and attempts to take down a mob ring.

Carrie (1952)

Starring: Laurence Olivier, Jennifer Jones, Miriam Hopkins. Director: William Wyler. Written by Ruth Goetz and Augustus Goetz, adapted from the novel (Sister Carrie) by Theodore Dreiser; 118 minutes; Paramount Pictures. A farm girl moves to Chicago and falls for a married man; later, she attempts to realize her dreams of Broadway fame.

Cavalcade (1933)

Starring: Diana Wynyard, Clive Brook. Director: Frank Lloyd. Written by Reginald Berkeley, adapted from the play by Noel Coward; 110 minutes; Fox Films Corporation. In this adaptation of the Noel Coward play, two British families live through such upheavals as Queen Victoria's death, the Boer War, and World War I, never losing hope despite their constantly shifting fortunes.

Children of a Lesser God (1986)

Starring: William Hurt, Marlee Matlin, Piper Laurie. Director: Randa Haines. Written by Hesper Anderson, adapted from the play by Mark Medoff; 119 minutes; Paramount Pictures. A speech teacher falls in love with a deaf custodian at the school where he works, trying to teach her to speak despite her resistance against the callous outer world.

A Christmas Carol (1951)

Starring: Alastair Sim. Director: Brian Desmond Hurst. Written by Noel Langley, adapted from the story by Charles Dickens; 86 minutes; George Minter Productions. After being haunted by several ghosts who present to him his past mistakes, Ebenezer Scrooge transforms from a miser to a charitable man.

Circle of Danger (1951)

Starring: Ray Milland, Patricia Roc, Marius Goring. Director: Jacques Tourneur. Written by Philip MacDonald, adapted from the novel by Philip MacDonald; 86 minutes; United Artists. An American travels to England to discover the circumstances surrounding his brother's death during World War II, eventually confronting his brother's killer.

Citizen Kane (1941)

Starring: Orson Welles, William Alland. Director: Orson Welles. Written by Orson Welles and Herman J. Mankiewicz; 119 minutes; Mercury Productions Inc. Classic film in which a journalist attempts to document the rise and fall—and the unanswered questions—of a newspaper tycoon's life.

Cocoon (1985)

Starring: Don Ameche, Wilford Brimley, Hume Cronyn. Director: Ron Howard. Written by Tom Benedek and David Saperstein; 117 minutes; Twentieth Century Fox. A group of elderly people find themselves enjoying newly youthful bodies after a swim in a pool full of alien cocoons.

Contact (1997)

Starring: Jodie Foster, Matthew McConaughey. Director: Robert Zemeckis. Written by James V. Hart and Michael Goldenberg, adapted from the novel by Carl Sagan; 153 minutes; Warner Brothers Pictures. An astronomer, having been contacted by aliens through radio waves, works with the government to build a giant machine to communicate with them.

Croupier (1998)

Starring: Clive Owen, Nick Reding. Director: Mike Hodges. Written by Paul Mayersberg; 94 minutes; Channel Four Films. A novelist takes a job at a posh London gaming club that quickly becomes fodder for his writing.

The Cruel Sea (1953)

Starring: Jack Hawkins, Donald Sinden, John Stratton. Director: Charles Frend. Written by Eric Ambler, adapted from the novel by Nicholas Monsarrat; 126 minutes; Ealing Studios. The veteran of a U-boat attack must decide between destroying a German boat or saving the lives of his inexperienced crew.

Dances with Wolves (1990)

Starring: Kevin Costner, Mary McDonnell, Graham Greene. Director: Kevin Costner. Written by Michael Blake; 180 minutes; Tig Productions. A former Union soldier renounces American culture and makes a new life among nature, animals, and Indians.

Daybreak (1939)

Starring: Jean Gabin, Jules Berry, Jacqueline Laurent. Director: Marcel Carné. Written by Jacques Prévert; 96 minutes; Sigma. To defend his honor, a man must kill the man who tried to seduce his lover. Following the murder, he is forced to analyze his life and the choices that brought him to his current situation.

The Defiant Ones (1958)

Starring: Tony Curtis, Sidney Poitier, Theodore Bikel. Director: Stanley Kramer. Written by Nedrick Young and Harold Jacob Smith; 97 minutes; Curtleigh Productions Inc. In order to survive and maintain their newfound freedom, two convicts handcuffed together are forced to cooperate with each other.

Deliverance (1972)

Starring: Jon Voight, Burt Reynolds, Ned Beatty. Director: John Boorman. Written by James Dickey; 109 minutes; Warner Bros. Pictures. An adaptation of the James Dickey novel about a group of friends who take a trip down a notoriously dangerous river, encountering a group of animalistic hicks.

The Detective (1968)

Starring: Frank Sinatra, Lee Remick, Ralph Meeker. Director: Gordon Douglas. Written by Abby Mann, adapted from the novel by Roderick Thorp; 114 minutes; Twentieth Century Fox. A detective investigating the murder of a young gay man discovers evidence pointing to rampant police corruption.

Detour (1945)

Starring: Tom Neal, Ann Savage, Claudia Drake. Director: Edgar G. Ulmer. Written by Martin Goldsmith; 67 minutes; Producers Releasing Corporation. A desperate drifter hitchhiking across American and searching for his girlfriend finds himself caught in a crime of identity theft.

The D.I. (1957)

Starring: Jack Webb, Don Dubbins, Jackie Loughery. Director: Jack Webb. Written by James Lee Barrett; 106 minutes; Mark VII Ltd. A young recruit threatens the power of a tough drill sergeant.

Diabolique (1955)

Starring: Simone Signoret, Vera Clouzot, Paul Meurisse. Director: H. G. Clouzot; Written by Jérôme Géronimi, Frédéric Grendel, and René Masson; 114 minutes; Filmsonor S.A. Together, two women plot to kill a man: a headmaster who is married to one of the women and having an affair with the other.

The Diary of Anne Frank (1959)

Starring: Millie Perkins, Joseph Schildkraut, Shelley Winters. Director: George Stevens. Written by Frances Goodrich and Albert Hackett, adapted from the book by Anne Frank; 180 minutes; Twentieth Century Fox. While eluding Nazis and hiding out with her family in an attic, a young Jewish girl falls in love with a fellow fugitive and meets a tragic end.

Dillinger (1945)

Starring: Lawrence Tierney, Edmund Lowe. Director: Max Nosseck. Written by Philip Yordan; 70 minutes; King Brothers Productions. Biopic that follows the rise of a small-time criminal, John Dillinger, as he becomes the quintessential American gangster through robberies, murders, and jailbreaks.

Dirty Harry (1971)

Starring: Clint Eastwood, Andy Robinson. Director: Don Siegel. Written by Harry Julian Fink, R. M. Fink, and Dean Reisner; 102 minutes; The Malpaso Company. A detective from San Francisco takes the law into his own hands as he hunts down a serial killer nicknamed "The Scorpio."

Dodsworth (1936)

Starring: Walter Huston, Ruth Chatterton. Director: William Wyler. Written by Sidney Howard; 101 minutes; Samuel Goldwyn Company. A self-made automobile tycoon begins to distance himself from his snobby wife after she reveals her attraction to another man.

Door to Door (2002)

Starring: William H. Macy, Helen Mirren, Kyra Sedgwick. Director: Steven Schachter. Written by William H. Macy and Steven Schachter; 90 minutes; Angel/Brown Productions. Despite the odds, a man suffering from cerebral palsy refuses charity and becomes a door-to-door salesman.

Dr. No (1962)

Starring: Sean Connery, Ursula Andress, Joseph Wiseman. Director: Terence Young. Written by Richard Maibaum, Johannah Harwood, and Berkely Mather, adapted from the novel by Ian Fleming; 110 minutes; Eon Productions Ltd. In this, the first James Bond movie, the British agent is sent to Jamaica to investigate a mysterious scientist and his involvement in the murder of a fellow spy.

Dr. Strangelove (1964)

Starring: Orson Welles, George C. Scott. Director: Stanley Kubrick. Written by Stanley Kubrick, Terry Southern, and Peter George; 93 minutes; Hawk Films Ltd. A black comedy about a general who announces his plans to start a nuclear war in a room full of politicians.

The Dukes of Hazzard (2005)

Starring: Johnny Knoxville, Sean William Scott, Jessica Simpson. Director: Jay Chandrasekhar. Written by John O'Brien and Jonathan L. Davis; 106 minutes; Gerber Pictures. A family of hillbillies constantly provokes members of law enforcement, who plot their revenge by trying to take the family's farm.

Dumbo (1941)

Director: Ben Sharpsteen. Written by Otto Englander, Helen Aberson, Joe Grant, and Dick Huemer; 64 minutes; Walt Disney Pictures. Due to his enormous ears, a circus elephant becomes an outcast, but with the help of a friend he learns what he is truly capable of.

The Entertainer (1960)

Starring: Laurence Olivier, Brenda De Banzie, Roger Livesey. Director: Tony Richardson. Written by Nigel Kneale and John Osborne; 96 minutes;

Woodfall Film Prodcutions. When things in his life start to come apart, a mediocre performer has no choice but to put on a good show at the seaside resort where he works.

Erin Brockovich (2000)

Starring: Julia Roberts, Aaron Eckhart, Albert Finney. Director: Steven Soderbergh. Written by Susannah Grant; 130 minutes; Jersey Films. A single mother of three takes a job as a legal secretary. After meeting several clients suffering from cancer and other illnesses, she begins to investigate a power company for illegal pollution of water.

Exodus (1960)

Starring: Paul Newman, Eva Marie Saint. Director: Otto Preminger. Written by Dalton Trumbo; 208 minutes; Carlyle Productions. A look at the founding and early days of Israel after the end of World War II, focusing on an Israeli resistance member who attempts to relocate six hundred Jews from Cyprus to Palestine.

Fahrenheit 9/11 (2004)

Director: Michael Moore. Written by Michael Moore; 122 minutes; Lions Gate Films. Documentary filmmaker Michael Moore's look at post–9/11 America and how the Bush Administration has manipulated this national tragedy to push forward a conservative political agenda.

Fail-Safe (1964)

Starring: Dan O'Herlihy, Walter Matthau. Director: Sidney Lumet. Written by Walter Bernstein, adapted from the novel by Eugene Burdick and Harvey Wheeler; 112 minutes; Columbia Pictures Corporation. An American air squadron is mistakenly sent to bomb Russia, forcing the American president to contemplate shooting down all the pilots in an attempt to stop them.

The Fatal Glass of Beer (1933)

Starring: W. C. Fields, Rosemary Thelby, George Chandler. Director: Clyde Bruckman. Written by W. C. Fields; 21 minutes; Mack Sennett. After leaving the Yukon to go to the big city, where he was briefly imprisoned, a young man returns home to his parents.

Flightplan (2005)

Starring: Jodie Foster, Peter Sarsgaard. Director: Robert Schwentke. Written by Peter A. Dowling and Billy Ray; 98 minutes; Touchstone Pictures. Flying home after the tragic death of her husband, a woman wakes up and realizes her daughter has disappeared mid-flight.

Forrest Gump (1994)

Starring: Tom Hanks, Robin Wright, Gary Sinise. Director: Robert Zemeckis. Written by Eric Roth, adapted from the novel by Winston Groom; 142 minutes; Paramount Pictures. A man born with a low IQ and leg problems makes his mark on American history, all the while pining for his childhood love, Jenny.

49th Parallel (1941)

Starring: Richard George, Eric Portman, Raymond Lovell. Director: Michael Powell. Written by Emeric Pressburger and Rodney Ackland; 123 minutes; Ortus Films Ltd. After sinking off the coast of Canada, the crew of a German U-boat has to flee to the neutral United States.

42nd Street (1933)

Starring: Warner Baxter, Bebe Daniels. Director: Lloyd Bacon. Written by Rian James and James Seymour, adapted from the novel by Bradford Ropes; 89 minutes; Warner Bros. Pictures. This twist on the classic Cinderella story has an average understudy take the place of the star in a Broadway show.

Friday the 13th (1980)

Starring: Betsy Palmer, Kevin Bacon. Director: Sean S. Cunningham. Written by Victor Miller; 95 minutes; Paramount Pictures. At a newly reopened summer camp, several counselors are murdered in a particularly gruesome fashion.

The Friends of Eddie Coyle (1973)

Starring: Robert Mitchum, Peter Boyle, Richard Jordan. Director: Peter Yates. Written by Paul Monash, adapted from the novel by George V. Higgins; 102 minutes; Paramount Pictures. On the eve of going to jail, a gangster agrees to supply guns for a bank robbery, planning to use the profits to provide for his wife while he is in jail.

The Front Page (1931)

Starring: Adolphe Menjou, Pat O'Brien, Mary Brian. Director: Lewis Milestone. Written by Bartlett Cormack, adapted from the play by Ben Hecht and Charles MacArthur; 101 minutes; The Caddo Company. A reporter planning to marry his fiancée faces opposition from his editor, who wants him to stay on.

Galaxy Quest (1999)

Starring: Tim Allen, Sigourney Weaver, Alan Rickman. Director: Dean Parisot. Written by David Howard and Robert Gordon; 102 minutes; DreamWorks SKG. While attending a sci-fi convention, the cast of a cult TV show find themselves beamed up by aliens who mistake them for actual space explorers.

General della Rovere (1959)

Starring: Vittorio De Sica, Hannes Messemer, Vittorio Caprioli. Director: Roberto Rossellini. Written by Sergio Amidei and Diego Fabbri; 129 minutes; Société Nouvelle des Établissements Gaumont (SNEG). After being arrested by the Nazis during the occupation of Italy, a swindler must pretend to be a recently executed Italian general.

Gentleman Jim (1942)

Starring: Errol Flynn, Alexis Smith, Jack Carson. Director: Raoul Walsh. Written by Vincent Lawrence, Horace McCoy, and James J. Corbett; 104 minutes; Warner Bros. Pictures. Biopic of boxer Jim Corbett, or "Gentleman Jim," who rose from meager beginnings to become the first heavyweight champion.

Gentleman's Agreement (1947)

Starring: Gregory Peck, Dorothy McGuire, John Garfield. Director: Elia Kazan. Written by Moss Hart, adapted from the novel by Laura Z. Hobson; 118 minutes; Twentieth Century Fox Film Corporation. In order to fully uncover the extent of anti-Semitism, a journalist claims to be Jewish and then writes an article about his experiences.

The Godfather (1972)

Starring: Marlon Brando, Al Pacino, James Caan. Director: Francis Ford Coppola. Written by Mario Puzo and Francis Ford Coppola; 175 minutes; Paramount Pictures. After years as the head of an organized crime syndicate, a powerful mob mogul passes power to an unlikely and unwilling son after an attack on his life.

The Godfather, Part II (1974)

Starring: Al Pacino, Robert Duvall, Diane Keaton. Director: Francis Ford Coppola. Written by Mario Puzo and Francis Ford Coppola; 200 minutes; Paramount Pictures. In this sequel to *The Godfather*, Vito Corleone's early life and rise to power is told in detail. Meanwhile, in the present day his son increases his control over his father's dynasty.

Godzilla *(1954)*

Starring: Akira Takarada, Momoko Kôchi. Director: Ishirô Honda. Written by Ishirô Honda, Takeo Murata, and Shigeru Kayama; 98 minutes; Toho Film (Eiga) Co. Ltd. A huge reptilian monster, created after nuclear weapons testing, terrorizes Japan.

Gold of Naples *(1954)*

Starring: Silvana Mangano, Sophia Loren. Director: Vittorio De Sica. Written by Vittorio De Sica, Giuseppe Marotta, and Cesare Zavattini; 131 minutes; Pomti–De Laurentiis Cinematografica. Film composed of six vignettes highlighting contemporary life in Naples.

Gone With the Wind *(1939)*

Starring: Clark Gable, Vivien Leigh. Director: Victor Fleming. Written by Sidney Howard, adapted from the novel by Margaret Mitchell; 222 minutes; Selznick International Pictures. A Southern belle, desperate to get the man she wants, meets and eventually marries a charming but ungentlemanly man.

Grand Illusion *(1937)*

Starring: Jean Gabin, Eric von Stroheim, Pierre Fresnay. Director: Jean Renoir. Written by Jean Renoir and Charles Spaak; 114 minutes; R.A.C. (Réalisation d'art cinématographique). In one of the earliest prison-break movies, three men attempt to escape a German POW camp during World War I.

The Greatest Story Ever Told *(1965)*

Starring: Max von Sydow, Michael Anderson Jr., Carroll Baker. Director: George Stevens. Written by James Lee Barrett and George Stevens; 225 minutes; George Stevens Productions. Epic biopic that follows the birth, life, and death of Jesus Christ.

The Green Mile *(1999)*

Starring: Tom Hanks, David Morse, Michael Clarke Duncan. Director: Frank Darabont. Written by Frank Darabont, adapted from the novel by Stephen King; 188 minutes; Castle Rock Entertainment. Several prison guards are forced to reconsider their racist views after discovering an innocent man on death row has the healing touch.

Guess Who's Coming to Dinner (1967)
    Starring: Spencer Tracy, Katharine Hepburn, Sidney Poitier. Director: Stanley Kramer. Written by William Rose; 108 minutes; Stanley Kramer Productions. Classic film in which an affluent white couple are shocked when they discover that their daughter plans to marry a black man.

Gun Crazy (1949)
    Starring: Peggy Cummins, John Dall. Director: Joseph H. Lewis. Written by MacKinlay Kantor and Dalton Trumbo; 86 minutes; King Bros. Productions Inc. A young gun-obsessed man and a female sharpshooter fall in love and take off on a crime spree.

Hail the Conquering Hero (1944)
    Starring: Eddie Bracken, Ella Raines. Director: Preston Sturges. Written by Preston Sturges; 101 minutes; Paramount Pictures. Several Marines pass off a blue-collar friend as the hero of Guadalcanal and watch as his hometown celebrates their most famous citizen.

Halloween (1978)
    Starring: Donald Pleasence, Jamie Lee Curtis. Director: John Carpenter. Written by John Carpenter and Debra Hill; 91 minutes; Compass International Pictures. After breaking out of a mental hospital, an insane murderer returns to the town where he killed his sister years before.

Here Comes Mr. Jordan (1941)
    Starring: Robert Montgomery, Evelyn Keyes. Director: Alexander Hall. Written by Sidney Buchman and Seton I. Miller, adapted from the play (*Heaven Can Wait*) by Harry Segall; 94 minutes; Columbia Pictures Corporations. When heaven makes a mistake and calls up boxer Joe Pendleton too early, Joe gets compensated by being reborn as a millionaire heartthrob.

High Noon (1952)
    Starring: Gary Cooper, Thomas Mitchell. Director: Fred Zinneman. Written by Carl Foreman and John W. Cunningham; 85 minutes; Stanley Kramer Procutions. On his wedding day, the town sheriff discovers an outlaw's plot to attack the town during the wedding. The sheriff has no choice but to appeal to the townspeople, who are reluctant to help.

Hoffa (1992)

Starring: Jack Nicholson, Danny DeVito, Armand Assante. Director: Danny DeVito. Written by David Mamet; 140 minutes; Twentieth Century Fox. Biopic based on the life of the famous union leader Jimmy Hoffa, including his battles with the government and the mysterious circumstances surrounding his disappearance.

Hollywoodism: Jews, Movies and the American Dream (1998)

Director: Simcha Jacobovici. Written by Simcha Jacobovici, adapted from the book (*An Empire of Their Own*) by Neal Gabler; 98 minutes; Canadian Broadcasting Corporation. An analysis of how Eastern European Jewish immigrants affected Hollywood in film's early years.

House of Games (1987)

Starring: Lindsay Crouse, Joe Mantegna, Mike Nussbaum. Director: David Mamet. Written by Jonathan Katz and David Mamet; 102 minutes; Filmhaus. A psychologist, attempting to help her patient break free of gambling debt, finds herself fascinated by the culture of the gambling house and its proprietor.

I Am a Fugitive from a Chain Gang (1932)

Starring: Paul Muni, Glenda Farrell, Helen Vinson. Director: Mervyn LeRoy. Written by Howard J. Green and Brown Holmes, adapted from the autobiographical book by Robert E. Burns; 93 minutes; The Vitaphone Corporation. An innocent man is haunted by his life in the prison system and terrorized by his time on a chain gang.

I Know Where I'm Going! (1945)

Starring: Wendy Hiller, Roger Livesey. Director: Michael Powell and Emeric Pressburger. Written by Michael Powell and Emeric Pressburger; 88 minutes; Rank Organisation. On the way to her wedding, a British woman finds herself stranded on an island in the Hebrides with a naval officer.

The Ice Storm (1997)

Starring: Kevin Kline, Joan Allen, Sigourney Weaver. Director: Ang Lee. Written by James Schamus, adapted from the novel by Rick Moody; 112 minutes; Fox Searchlight Pictures. The craziness of the 1970s reaches suburbia, as a pair of middle-class families walk down the path of sex, drugs, and alcohol, only to discover that they have lost control over their children.

I'll Cry Tomorrow (1955)

Starring: Susan Hayward, Richard Conte, Eddie Albert. Director: Daniel Mann. Written by Helen Deutsch and Jay Richard Kennedy, adapted from the book by Lillian Roth, Mike Connolly, and Gerold Frank; 117 minutes; Metro-Goldwyn-Mayer (MGM). After being forced by her mother into acting, a starlet's personal life crumbles as she becomes dependent on drugs and men.

I'll Sleep When I'm Dead (2003)

Starring: Clive Owen, Charlotte Rampling, Jonathan Rhys Meyers. Director: Mike Hodges. Written by Trevor Preston; 103 minutes; Revere Pictures. A former mobster searches with his ex-girlfriend for his brother's murderer, jeopardizing his dream of a quiet, crime-free life.

In Which We Serve (1942)

Starring: Noel Coward, John Mills, Bernard Miles. Director: Noel Coward and David Lean. Written by Noel Coward; 115 minutes; Two Cities Films Ltd. Classic film depicting three crew members of a British battleship who are marooned on a life raft in the Mediterranean.

Intolerance: Love's Struggle Throughout the Ages (1916)

Starring: Mae Marsh, Robert Harron, Fred Turner. Director: D.W. Griffith. Written by D.W. Griffith; 163 minutes; Triangle Film Corporation. Silent film that explores intolerance from preclassical times to contemporary America.

It's a Mad Mad Mad Mad World (1963)

Starring: Spencer Tracy, Milton Berle, Sid Caesar. Director: Stanley Kramer. Written by William Rose and Tania Rose; 192 minutes; Casey Productions. A policeman chases after several money-hungry people, all of whom are seeking a dead thief's buried treasure.

It's a Wonderful Life (1946)

Starring: James Stewart, Donna Reed. Director: Frank Capra. Written by Frances Goodrich, Albert Hackett, and Frank Capra; 130 minutes; Liberty Films Inc. An unbelievably good man whose business is failing gets a look at what life would be like if he had never been born.

Jaws (1975)

Starring: Roy Scheider, Robert Shaw, Richard Dreyfuss. Director: Steven Spielberg. Written by Peter Benchley; 124 minutes; Universal Pictures. After a shark threatens a local beach, a police chief, a shark hunter, and an oceanographer set out on a quest to kill it.

The Jazz Singer (1927)

Starring: Al Jolson, May McAvoy, Warner Oland. Director: Alan Crosland. Written by Alfred A. Cohn, adapted from the play by Samson Raphaelson; 88 minutes; Warner Bros. Pictures. A young man fulfills his dreams of becoming a jazz singer while going against his father's wishes.

Jolson Sings Again (1949)

Starring: Larry Parks, Barbara Hale, William Demarest. Director: Henry Levin. Written by Sidney Buchman; 96 minutes; Columbia Pictures Corporation. A continuation of Al Jolson's life from The Jolson Story, this film shows the singer's career as he comes out of retirement.

The Jolson Story (1946)

Starring: Larry Parks, Evelyn Keyes, William Demarest. Director: Alfred E. Green. Written by Stephen Longstreet; 128 minutes; Columbia Pictures Corporation. Biopic that follows Al Jolson, a celebrated performer who experienced unparalleled success, through the ups and downs of his life.

The Joy Luck Club (1993)

Starring: Kieu Chinh, Tsai Chin, France Nuyen. Director: Wayne Wang. Written by Amy Tan and Ronald Bass; 139 minutes; Hollywood Pictures. Multigenerational story about four Chinese women who were raised in a male-dominated culture and their American daughters who have led very different lives.

Khartoum (1966)

Starring: Charlton Heston, Laurence Olivier. Director: Basil Dearden, Eliot Elisofon. Written by Robert Ardrey; 134 minutes; Julian Blaustein Productions Ltd. Set in the 1830s during the British defeat in North Africa, the film follows a Christian general who disregards orders and battles the invading Arab forces.

The Killing (1956)

Starring: Sterling Hayden, Coleen Gray, Vince Edwards. Director: Stanley Kubrick. Written by Stanley Kubrick, adapted from the novel (Clean Break) by Lionel White; 85 minutes; Harris-Kubrick Productions. Upon his release from jail, a criminal attempts to rob a racetrack only to have his plan foiled.

King of Marvin Gardens (1972)

Starring: Jack Nicholson, Bruce Dern, Ellen Burstyn. Director: Bob Rafelson. Written by Jacob Brackman and Bob Rafelson; 103 minutes; BBS Productions. A man goes to Atlantic City to help his brother escape from jail through a series of well-played cons.

Kiss the Blood off My Hands (1948)

Starring: Joan Fontaine, Burt Lancaster, Robert Newton. Director: Norman Foster. Written by Leonardo Bercovici; 79 minutes; Norma Productions Inc. A nurse gets the shock of her life when she discovers a fugitive hiding out in her apartment.

Knute Rockne All American (1940)

Starring: Pat O'Brien, Gale Page. Director: Lloyd Bacon. Written by Robert Buckner; 98 minutes; First National Pictures Inc. A biopic of the famous Notre Dame football coach Knute Rockne and his innovative strategies that allowed Notre Dame to dominate the sport.

The Krays (1990)

Starring: Billie Whitelaw, Tom Bell, Gary Kemp, Martin Kemp. Director: Peter Medak. Written by Philip Ridley; 119 minutes; Parkfield Entertainment. Twin brothers rule organized crime with iron fists in sixties London, but their violent ways come back to haunt them.

The Lady Eve (1941)

Starring: Barbara Stanwyck, Henry Fonda, Charles Coburn. Director: Preston Sturges. Written by Preston Sturges and Monckton Hoffe; 97 minutes; Paramount Pictures. After a failed love affair, a con artist terrorizes a dimwitted, but incredibly wealthy, man, inadvertently falling in love with him as he discovers her scheme.

The Last Temptation of Christ (1988)

Starring: Willem Dafoe, Harvey Keitel, Verna Bloom. Director: Martin Scorsese. Written by Paul Schrader, adapted from the novel by Nikos Kazantzakis; 164 minutes; Universal Pictures. In this version of the story of Jesus Christ, Jesus is portrayed as an unwilling savior who is tempted to avoid his destiny by the possibility of life with Mary Magdalene.

A League of Their Own (1992)

Starring: Tom Hanks, Geena Davis, Madonna. Director: Penny Marshall. Story written by Kim Wilson, Kelly Candaele. Screenplay by Lowell Ganz and Babaloo Mandel; 128 minutes; Columbia Pictures Corporation. Two small-town sisters become stars in a woman's baseball league created during World War II, coached by a former superstar who is deeply scarred after years of heavy drinking.

The Life and Death of Colonel Blimp (1943)

Starring: James McKechnie, Neville Mapp, Vincent Holman. Director: Michael Powell and Emeric Pressburger. Written by Michael Powell and Emeric Pressburger; 163 minutes; Independent Producers. After a lifetime in military service, a retired general looks back on four decades of fighting, three wars, and multiple romances.

Life With Father (1947)

Starring: William Powell, Irene Dunne, Elizabeth Taylor. Director: Michael Curtiz. Written by Howard Lindsay and Russel Crouse, adapted from the book by Clarence Day; 128 minutes; Warner Bros. Pictures. An adaptation of Clarence Day's nostalgic memoir about the man who shaped his adolescence: his father, who ran his family like a company.

Lock, Stock, and Two Smoking Barrels (1998)

Starring: Jason Flemyng, Jason Statham, Vinnie Jones. Director: Guy Ritchie. Written by Guy Ritchie; 108 minutes; Polygram Filmed Entertainment. Four Londoners are forced to steal from thieves after losing a high-stakes poker game to a high-ranking mobster.

The Long Good Friday (1980)

Starring: Bob Hoskins, Helen Mirren, Dave King. Director: John MacKenzie. Written by Barrie Keeffe; 109 minutes; Black Lion Films Limited. As a new generation of gangsters rises to power, an underworld boss must fight off the competition.

The Magnificent Ambersons (1942)

Starring: Joseph Cotton, Dolores Costello, Anne Baxter. Director: Orson Welles. Written by Orson Welles, adapted from the novel by Booth Tarkington; 148 minutes; Mercury Productions Inc. As his once-wealthy family declines, a man plots to marry his first love after the death of his wife, much to the chagrin of his son.

Masada (miniseries, 1981)
   Starring: Peter O'Toole, Peter Strauss. Director: Boris Segal. Written by Joel Oliansky and Ernest K. Gann; 394 minutes; Arnon Milchan Productions. A Roman commander hoping to compromise with the local Jewish population finds his fortress under attack.

The Matrix (1999)
   Starring: Keanu Reeves, Laurence Fishburne, Carrie-Anne Moss. Directors: Andy Wachowski and Larry Wachowski. Written by Andy Wachowski and Larry Wachowski; 136 minutes; Silver Pictures. A group of leather-clad rebels attempts to show a computer geek the true nature of the world in an effort to defeat their robotic captors.

The Miracle of Morgan's Creek (1944)
   Starring: Eddie Bracken, Betty Hutton, Diana Lynn. Director: Preston Sturges. Written by Preston Sturges; 99 minutes; Paramount Pictures. A farcical story about a woman who finds herself pregnant and clueless as to who the father is after an all-night party.

Miracle on 34th Street (1947)
   Starring: Maureen O'Hara, John Payne, Edmund Gwenn. Director: George Seaton. Written by George Seaton and Valentine Davies; 96 minutes; Twentieth Century Fox Film Corporation. Heartwarming tale about a young girl whose faith in the existence of Santa Claus is restored as she befriends an old man who claims to be Kris Kringle himself.

Mona Lisa (1986)
   Starring: Bob Hoskins, Cathy Tyson, Michael Caine. Director: Neil Jordan. Written by Neil Jordan and David Leland; 104 minutes; Handmade Films Ltd. George, a criminal with a sense of morals searching for a job after being released from prison, gets a job as the chauffeur of a pricey call girl.

The Narrow Margin (1952)
   Starring: Charles McGraw, Marie Windsor, Jacqueline White. Director: Richard Fleischer. Written by Earl Felton, Martin Goldsmith, and Jack Leonard; 71 minutes; RKO Radio Pictures. The widow of a mobster is planning to testify at a grand jury despite several death threats; a hard-nosed detective is assigned to escort her as she makes the train trip from Chicago to Los Angeles, where she will give testimony.

New Orleans *(1947)*

Starring: Arturo De Cordova, Dorothy Patrick, Marjorie Lord, Billie Holiday. Director: Arthur Lubin. Written by Elliot Paul, Dick Irving Hyland, and Herbert J. Biberman; 90 minutes; Majestic Productions Inc. As jazz begins to captivate America, a gambler falls for a wealthy woman who attempts to reform him into respectability.

Night and the City *(1950)*

Starring: Richard Widmark, Gene Tierney, Googie Withers. Director: Jules Dassin. Written by Jo Eisenger, adapted from the novel by Gerald Kirsh; 101 minutes; Twentieth Century Fox Productions Ltd. A lawyer seduces the wife of an old friend who is too busy to notice, as he is trying to scam everyone he knows.

Not a Love Story: A Film About Pornography *(1981)*

Director: Bonnie Sherr Klein. Written by Andrée Klein, Bonnie Sherr Klein, Irene Lilienheim Angelico, and Rose-Aimée Todd; 70 minutes; National Film Board of Canada (NFB). Documentary that examines the misogynistic practices of American pornography culture.

Now, Voyager *(1942)*

Starring: Bette Davis, Paul Henreid, Claude Rains. Director: Irving Rapper. Written by Casey Robinson, adapted from the novel by Olive Higgins Prouty; 117 minutes; Warner Bros. Pictures. An ugly spinster transforms into a beautiful young lady through therapy, leading her down the path toward love.

One Million B.C. *(1940)*

Starring: Victor Mature, Carole Landis, Lon Chaney Jr. Director: Hal Roach and Hal Roach Jr. Written by Mickell Novack, George Baker, and Joseph Frickert; 80 minutes; Hal Roach Studios Inc. After being exiled by his tribe, a prehistoric man finds a new home where he learns manners.

One of Our Aircraft Is Missing *(1942)*

Starring: Godfrey Tearle, Eric Portman, Hugh Williams. Director: Michael Powell and Emeric Pressburger. Written by Michael Powell and Emeric Pressburger; 103 minutes; British National Films Ltd. After being shot down over Holland, a Royal Air Force crew must escape to England before being found by the Nazis.

Only Angels Have Wings (1939)

Starring: Cary Grant, Jean Arthur. Director: Howard Hawks. Written by Jules Furthman and Howard Hawks; 121 minutes; Columbia Pictures Corporation. An air squadron commander strikes up a relationship with a glamorous woman in South America after dismissing her husband from the squad.

The Ox-Bow Incident (1943)

Starring: Henry Fonda, Dana Andrews, Mary Beth Hughes. Director: William A. Wellman. Written by Lamar Trotti, adapted from the novel by Walter Van Tilburg Clark; 75 minutes; Twentieth Century Fox Film Corporation. After discovering the innocence of three men about to be lynched, a pair of drifters attempts to stop the execution.

Panic Room (2002)

Starring: Jodie Foster, Kristen Stewart, Forest Whitaker. Director: David Fincher. Written by David Koepp; 112 minutes; Columbia Pictures Corporation. One night in a new house, a woman and her daughter are forced to hide in a "panic room" as three men search their house for money.

The Passion of the Christ (2004)

Starring: James Caviezel, Maia Morgenstern, Hristo Jivkov. Director: Mel Gibson. Written by Benedict Fitzgerald and Mel Gibson; 126 minutes; Icon Productions. A brutally detailed account of the last hours and the death of Jesus Christ.

Paths of Glory (1957)

Starring: Kirk Douglas, Ralph Meeker, Adolphe Menjou. Director: Stanley Kubrick. Written by Stanley Kubrick, Calder Willingham, and Jim Thompson, adapted from the novel by Humphrey Cobb; 86 minutes; Bryna Productions. After an officer leads his men into a battle that they have no chance of winning, he must defend several of his men against attacks of desertion and cowardice.

Peeping Tom (1960)

Starring: Carol Böhm, Moira Shearer, Anna Massey. Director: Michael Powell. Written by Leo Marks; 101 minutes; Anglo-Amalgamated Productions. An insane killer gains notoriety for photographing the last expressions of his dying victims.

Penny Serenade (1941)

Starring: Irene Dunne, Cary Grant. Director: George Stevens. Written by Morrie Ryskind and Martha Cheavens; 117 minutes; Columbia Pictures Corporation. As a woman prepares to abandon her husband, she remembers their struggles to have children and listens to the music that characterized their relationship.

Pillow Talk (1959)

Starring: Rock Hudson, Doris Day, Tony Randall. Director: Michael Gordon. Written by Maurice Richlin, Stanley Shapiro, Russell Rouse, and Clarence Greene; 98 minutes; Universal International Pictures. Two combative neighbors share a phone line; as a prank, the man begins to court the woman using a disguised voice.

The Pink Panther (1963)

Starring: Peter Sellers, Robert Wagner, David Niven. Director: Blake Edwards. Written by Maurice Richlin and Blake Edwards; 113 minutes; Geoffrey Productions Inc. An incompetent French detective hunts for a jewel thief who has stolen a famous diamond known as the Pink Panther.

A Place in the Sun (1951)

Starring: Montgomery Clift, Elizabeth Taylor, Shelley Winters. Director: George Stevens. Written by Michael Wilson and Harry Brown, adapted from the play *An American Tragedy* by Patrick Kearney and the novel of the same name by Theodore Dreiser; 122 minutes; Paramount Pictures. George, a blue-collar factory worker, begins a passionate relationship with a coworker, but after leaving her for a wealthy, beautiful woman, his spurned lover decides she wants him back.

Playing for Time (1980)

Starring: Vanessa Redgrave, Jane Alexander, Maud Adams. Director: Daniel Mann. Written by Arthur Miller, adapted from the autobiography *The Musicians of Auschwitz* by Fania Fénelon; 105 minutes; Szygzy Productions. A group of female prisoners at Auschwitz forms an orchestra and performs for the Nazis in order to save themselves from the Final Solution.

Plunder Road (1957)

Starring: Gene Raymond, Jeanne Cooper, Wayne Morris. Director: Hubert Cornfield. Written by Steven Ritch and Jack Charney; 76 minutes; Regal Films Inc. Five men attempt to flee across the country with $10 million from a train robbery that's on the front page of every newspaper.

Point Blank (1967)

Starring: Lee Marvin, Angie Dickinson, Keenan Wynn. Director: John Boorman. Written by Alexander Jacobs, David Newhouse, and Rafe Newhouse, adapted from the novel by Richard Stark; 92 minutes; Metro-Goldwyn-Mayer (MGM). A gangster is betrayed by his wife and his best friend, who leave him for dead; years later, he returns to exact revenge.

Porgy and Bess (1959)

Starring: Sidney Poitier, Dorothy Dandridge, Sammy Davis Jr. Director: Otto Preminger. Written by DuBose Heyward, Dorothy Heyward (both writers of the libretto for the play Porgy), and N. Richard Nash. 138 minutes; Samuel Goldwyn Company. A look at the beautiful but complicated relationship that emerges between the radiant Bess and the disabled Porgy, adapted from the Gershwin opera.

The Postman Always Rings Twice (1981)

Starring: Jack Nicholson, Jessica Lange, John Colicos. Director: Bob Rafelson. Written by David Mamet, adapted from the novel by James M. Cain; 122 minutes; CIP Filmproduktion GmbH. A young drifter begins to lust after a married woman, but their electric affair leads to murder.

The Pride of the Yankees (1942)

Starring: Gary Cooper, Teresa Wright, Babe Ruth. Director: Sam Wood. Written by Jo Swerling, Herman J. Mankiewicz, and Paul Gallico; 128 minutes; Samuel Goldwyn Company. A biopic portraying the life and decline of one of the most celebrated Yankees, Lou Gehrig, as he plays in more than two thousand consecutive games only to be felled by the illness now named after him.

Prince of the City (1981)

Starring: Treat Williams, Jerry Orbach, Richard Foronjy. Director: Sidney Lumet. Written by Jay Presson Allen and Sidney Lumet, adapted from the book by Robert Daley; 167 minutes; Orion. A New York City narcotics detective begins to work with Internal Affairs and uncovers widespread corruption in his department that implicates his friends.

Pygmalion (1938)

Starring: Leslie Howard, Wendy Hiller. Directors: Anthony Asquith, Leslie Howard. Written by W. P. Liscomb and Cecil Lewis, adapted from the play by George Bernard Shaw; 96 minutes; Gabriel Pascal Productions. A

cocky speech expert bets a friend that he can make a lower-class woman
into a proper lady in manner, dress, and speech.

The Quest for Fire (1981)

Starring: Everett McGill, Ron Perlman, Rae Dawn Chong. Director:
Jean-Jacques Annaud. Written by Gérard Brach, adapted from the novel by
J. H. Rosny Sr.; 100 minutes; Belstar Productions. A group of cavemen
attempt to master the creation of fire.

Quicksand (1950)

Starring: Mickey Rooney, Jeanne Cagney, Barbara Bates. Director: Irving Pichel. Written by Robert Smith; 79 minutes; Samuel H. Stiefel Productions. After stealing twenty dollars at work, a mechanic finds himself in
rapidly increasing debt as a disreputable carnival owner begin to extort him.

Rembrandt (1936)

Starring: Charles Laughton, Gertrude Lawrence, Elsa Lanchester. Director: Alexander Korda. Written by June Head, Lajos Biró, and Carl Zuck-
mayer; 86 minutes; London Film Productions. Biopic of the Dutch painter
as he struggles through personal tragedy late in his career, finding love in the
most unlikely of places.

Retreat, Hell! (1952)

Starring: Frank Lovejoy, Richard Carlson, Anita Louise. Director:
Joseph H. Lewis. Written by Ted Sherdeman and Milton Sperling; 94 minutes; United States Pictures. A group of American soldiers must fight against
impossible odds during the Korean War.

Rififi (1955)

Starring: Jean Servais, Carl Möhner, Robert Manuel. Director: Jules
Dassin. Written by Jules Dassin, René Wheeler, and Auguste Le Breton,
adapted from the novel by Auguste Le Breton; 115 minutes; Indusfilms. In a
classic case of the perfect crime gone wrong, four men map out a flawless
robbery only to have a woman put everything in turmoil.

The Rise and Fall of Legs Diamond (1960)

Starring: Ray Danton, Karen Steele, Elaine Steward. Director: Budd
Boetticher. Written by Joseph Landon; 101 minutes; United States Pictures.
Two low-life crooks rise to prominence by stealing from fellow criminals
during Prohibition.

Robbery (1967)

Starring: Stanley Baker, Joanna Pettet, James Booth. Director: Peter Yates. Written by Edward Boyd, George Markstein, Gerald Wilson, and Peter Yates; 110 minutes; Oakhurst Productions. A group of men create a detailed plan to rob the British Royal Mail train.

The Robe (1953)

Starring: Richard Burton, Jean Simmons, Victor Mature. Director: Henry Koster. Written by Gina Kaus, Albert Maltz, and Philip Dunne, adapted from the novel by Lloyd C. Douglas; 133 minutes; Twentieth Century Fox Film Corporation. After the execution of Jesus Christ, members of the Roman tribunal responsible for his death begin to have hallucinations that they believe are caused by Jesus' robe.

The Rules of the Game (1939)

Starring: Nora Grégor, Paulette Dubost, Mila Parély. Director: Jean Renoir., Written by Carl Koch; 143 minutes; Nouvelle edition française. When rich aristocrats and their poor servants camp out in a castle just before the World War II, the social tension builds, culminating in a murder.

Run Silent Run Deep (1958)

Starring: Clark Gable, Burt Lancaster, Jack Warden. Director: Robert Wise. Written by John Gay, adapted from the novel by Commander Edward L. Beach; 93 minutes; Hill-Hecht-Lancaster Productions. After a demotion, a U.S. submarine commander must learn to deal with his new boss as they hunt down a Japanese cruiser during World War II.

Sailor of the King (1953)

Starring: Jeffrey Hunter, Michael Rennie, Peter van Eyck. Director: Ray Boulting. Written by Valentine Davies, adapted from the novel by C. S. Forester; 85 minutes; Twentieth Century Fox Productions Ltd. In order to save his son, a British officer must make his way through the German army during World War II.

Sands of Iwo Jima (1949)

Starring: John Wayne, John Agar, Adele Mara. Director: Allen Dwan. Written by James Edward Grant and Harry Brown; 100 minutes; Republic Pictures Corporation. A notoriously tough sergeant attempts to keep his men alive during the epic World War II Battle of Iwo Jima.

Schindler's List (1993)

Starring: Liam Neeson, Ben Kingsley, Ralph Fiennes. Director: Steven Spielberg. Written by Steven Zaillian, adapted from the book by Thomas Keneally; 195 minutes; Amblin Entertainment. This drama retells the true story of Oskar Schindler, a factory owner who helped save the lives of hundreds of Polish Jews during World War II.

Sergeant York (1941)

Starring: Gary Cooper, Walter Brennan, Joan Leslie. Director: Howard Hawks. Written by Abem Finkel, Harry Chandlee, Howard Koch, and John Huston, based on a diary by Sergeant York; 134 minutes; Warner Bros. Pictures. A deeply religious country boy refuses to join the army, only to be drafted and become a decorated war hero.

Serpico (1973)

Starring: Al Pacino, John Randolph Jr., Jack Kehoe. Director: Sidney Lumet. Written by Waldo Salt and Norman Wexler, adapted from the book by Peter Maas; 129 minutes; Artists Entertainment Complex. A by-the-book cop in New York City uncovers and reveals departmental corruption, causing his former allies to become his enemies.

Sexy Beast (2000)

Starring: Ben Kingsley, Ray Winstone, Ian McShane. Director: Jonathan Glazer. Written by Louis Mellis and David Scinto; 89 minutes; FilmFour. Two gangsters find their peaceful retirement hindered by the return of an old friend who offers one last job.

The Shadow Box (1980)

Starring: Joanne Woodward, Christopher Plummer, Valerie Harper. Director: Paul Newman. Written by Michael Christofer; 96 minutes; Shadow Box Film Company. Adaptation of the play that depicts a day in the life of several terminally ill patients as they choose to live out their final moments in an experimental community.

Shadow of a Doubt (1943)

Starring: Teresa Wright, Joseph Cotton. Director: Alfred Hitchcock. Written by Thornton Wilder, Sally Benson, Alma Reville, and Gordon McDonnell; 108 minutes; Skirball Productions. A young girl, suspicious of her distant uncle, begins to suspect him of being a serial killer and attempts to reveal his crimes without raising suspicion.

The Sixth Sense (1999)

Starring: Bruce Willis, Haley Joel Osment, Toni Collette. Director: M. Night Shyamalan. Written by M. Night Shyamalan; 107 minutes; Barry Mendel Productions. Much to his mother's shock, as well as his own horror, a young boy realizes that he can see, hear, and speak with the dead.

Snatch (2000)

Starring: Brad Pitt, Jason Statham, Stephen Graham. Director: Guy Ritchie. Written by Guy Ritchie; 104 minutes; Columbia Pictures Corporation. Several less-than-competent criminals search for the stolen diamond that will make them rich beyond their wildest dreams.

Some Like it Hot (1959)

Starring: Marilyn Monroe, Jack Lemmon, Tony Curtis. Director: Billy Wilder. Written by Billy Wilder, I.A.L. Diamond, R. Thoeren, and M. Logan; 120 minutes; Ashton Productions. After witnessing a murder, two men go into hiding as the newest members of an all-girl band.

Sophie's Choice (1982)

Starring: Meryl Streep, Kevin Kline, Peter MacNicol. Director: Alan J. Pakula. Written by Alan J. Pakula, adapted from the novel by William Styron; 150 minutes; Incorporated Television Company (ITC). A woman attempts to hide her experiences during the Holocaust from two men who are deeply in love with her.

Spy Game (2001)

Starring: Robert Redford, Brad Pitt. Director: Tony Scott. Written by Michael Frost Beckner and David Arata; 126 minutes; Beacon Communications LLC. Moments from retirement, a CIA agent must risk everything to save his protégé from captivity.

State and Main (2000)

Starring: Alec Baldwin, Sarah Jessica Parker, William H. Macy, Philip Seymour Hoffman. Director: David Mamet. Written by David Mamet; 105 minutes; Filmtown Entertainment. In a dark look at fame-obsessed culture, a movie crew shakes up life in a sleepy New England town.

State of the Union (1948)

Starring: Spencer Tracy, Katharine Hepburn, Van Johnson. Director: Frank Capra. Written by Myles Connolly and Anthony Veiller, adapted from the play by Russel Crouse and Howard Lindsay; 124 minutes; Liberty Films Inc. A businessman, convinced by conniving politicians to enter a presidential race, starts speaking his own mind and ignoring the advice of his handlers.

Strategic Air Command (1955)

Starring: James Stewart, June Allyson. Director: Anthony Mann. Written by Valentine Davies and Beirne Lay Jr.; 114 minutes; Paramount Pictures. A celebrity baseball player gives it all up to serve his country.

The Sum of All Fears (2002)

Starring: Ben Affleck, Morgan Freeman, James Cromwell. Director: Phil Alden Robinson. Written by Paul Attanasio and Daniel Pyne, adapted from the novel by Tom Clancy; 124 minutes; Paramount Pictures. While the president attends the Super Bowl, a terrorist cell plans to set off a nuclear bomb at the event as a CIA agent tries to avert the crisis.

Sweet Smell of Success (1957)

Starring: Burt Lancaster, Tony Curtis, Susan Harrison. Director: Alexander Mackendrick. Written by Clifford Odets and Ernest Lehman; 96 minutes; Hill-Hecht-Lancaster Productions. A New York journalist uses a ruthless press agent in attempt to derail his sister's engagement before the wedding.

T-Men (1947)

Starring: Dennis O'Keefe, Mary Meade, Alfred Ryder. Director: Anthony Mann. Written by John C. Higgins and Virginia Kellogg; 92 minutes. Two agents from the United States Treasury infiltrate a counterfeiting ring with an unusually good talent for replicating actual currency.

Taxi Driver (1976)

Starring: Robert De Niro, Cybill Shepherd, Peter Boyle. Director: Martin Scorsese. Written by Paul Schrader; 113 minutes; Columbia Pictures Corporation. Isolated in New York City, a Vietnam vet takes it upon himself to violently liberate an adolescent prostitute from her pimp.

The Ten Commandments (1956)

Starring: Charlton Heston, Yul Brynner, Anne Baxter. Director: Cecil B. DeMille. Written by Æneas MacKenzie, Jesse Lasky Jr., Jack Gariss, and Fredric M. Frank; 220 minutes; Paramount Pictures. Based on the biblical story wherein Moses rises from slavery to lead his people to the promised land, Israel.

The Terminator (1984)

Starring: Arnold Schwarzenegger, Michael Biehn, Linda Hamilton. Director: James Cameron. Written by Gale Anne Hurd and James Cameron; 108 minutes; Hemdale Film Corporation. A futuristic man is sent from the future to save a woman and her son from a threatening, murderous cyborg.

That Hamilton Woman (1941)

Starring: Vivien Leigh, Laurence Olivier, Alan Mowbray. Director: Alexander Korda. Written by Walter Reisch and R. C. Sherriff; 128 minutes; Alexander Korda Films. A married socialite who's made the perfect match falls in love with a naval officer and becomes an outcast.

Thelma & Louise (1991)

Starring: Susan Sarandon, Geena Davis, Harvey Keitel. Director: Ridley Scott. Written by Callie Khouri; 129 minutes; Metro-Goldwyn-Mayer. Two friends, hoping to flee to Mexico after accidentally murdering an attempted rapist, bond as the authorities chase after them.

They Gave Him a Gun (1937)

Starring: Spencer Tracy, Gladys George, Franchot Tome. Director: W. S. Van Dyke II. Written by Cyril Hume, Richard Maibaum, and Maurice Rapf, adapted from the book by William Joyce Cowen; 94 minutes; Metro-Goldwyn-Mayer (MGM). During World War I, two soldiers realize they love the same woman, a nurse at the local base hospital.

Three Days of the Condor (1975)

Starring: Robert Redford, Faye Dunaway, Cliff Robertson. Director: Sydney Pollack. Written by Lorenzo Semple Jr. and David Rayfiel, adapted from the novel by James Grady; 117 minutes; Paramount Pictures. While taking part in an undercover investigation, a CIA agent finds his colleagues murdered and must run for his life.

Titanic (1997)

Starring: Leonardo DiCaprio, Kate Winslet, Billy Zane. Director: James Cameron. Written by James Cameron; 194 minutes; Twentieth Century Fox. While aboard the *Titanic* a wealthy girl engaged to a man she does not love becomes frustrated with her life and finds comfort in a lower-class man.

Training Day (2001)

Starring: Denzel Washington, Ethan Hawke, Scott Glenn. Director: Antoine Fuqua. Written by David Ayer; 120 minutes; Warner Bros. Pictures. A rookie cop discovers that the man training him is not merely an unorthodox detective but a vicious criminal.

Trapeze (1956)

Starring: Burt Lancaster, Tony Curtis, Gina Lollobrigida. Director: Carol Reed. Written by Liam O'Brien and James R. Webb, adapted from the novel (*The Killing Frost*) by Max Catto; 105 minutes; Hill-Hecht-Lancaster Productions. A former superstar acrobat who is past his prime takes on a protégé, only to have their budding friendship threatened by a woman.

The Triumph of the Will (1935)

Director: Leni Riefenstahl. Written by Leni Riefenstahl and Walter Ruttmann; 114 minutes; Leni Riefenstahl-Produktion. The infamous Nazi propaganda documentary centered on a rally in Nuremberg prior to the start of World War II.

Tunes of Glory (1960)

Starring: Alec Guinness, John Mills, Dennis Price. Director: Ronald Neame. Written by James Kennaway; 106 minutes; Knightsbridge Films. When a highly qualified general finds himself demoted and a younger man takes his position, a bitter rivalry quickly develops.

Twelve O'Clock High (1949)

Starring: Gregory Peck, Hugh Marlowe. Director: Henry King. Written by Sy Bartlett and Beirne Lay Jr.; 132 minutes; Twentieth Century Fox Film Corporation. In this Oscar-winning film set during World War II, a general takes over a British bomber division and inspires his men to victory, growing closer to them throughout their training.

The Untouchables (1987)

Starring: Kevin Costner, Sean Connery, Charles Martin Smith. Director: Brian De Palma. Written by David Mamet, adapted from the novel by Oscar Fraley and Eliot Ness; 119 minutes; Paramount Pictures. An elite squad of FBI agents attempts to arrest the legendary Chicago mob boss Al Capone.

Wag the Dog (1997)

Starring: Dustin Hoffman, Robert De Niro, Anne Heche. Director: Barry Levinson. Written by Hilary Henkin and David Mamet, adapted from the book (*American Hero*) by Larry Beinhart; 97 minutes; New Line Cinema. In order to divert the nation's attention from the president's molestation of a girl, a group of political consultants creates and televises a fake war.

The Wages of Fear (1953)

Starring: Yves Montand, Charles Vanel, Peter Van Eyck. Director: Henri-Georges Clouzot. Written by Henri-Georges Clouzot and Jérome Geronimi, adapted from the novel by Georges Arnaud; 148 minutes; CICC. In a small South American town, a crew is selected and paid to move nitroglycerine without proper safety equipment.

Whale Rider (2002)

Starring: Keisha Castle-Hughes, Rawiri Paratene, Vicky Haughton. Director: Niki Caro. Written by Niki Caro, adapted from the novel by Witi Ihimaera; 105 minutes; ApolloMedia. A young girl from a long line of whale riders breaks tradition to fulfill her dreams and become the leader of her Maori tribe.

Whose Life Is It Anyway? (1981)

Starring: Richard Dreyfuss, John Cassavetes, Christine Lahti. Director: John Badham. Written by Reginald Rose, adapted from the play by Brian Clark; 118 minutes; Metro-Goldwyn-Mayer (MGM). After a tragic accident leaves a brilliant and talented sculptor paralyzed, he argues for his right to be allowed to die.

Witness for the Prosecution (1957)

Starring: Tyrone Power, Marlene Dietrich, Charles Laughton. Director: Billy Wilder. Written by Larry Marcus, Billy Wilder, and Harry Kurnitz, adapted from the play by Agatha Christie; 116 minutes; Edward Small Productions. An aging lawyer is asked to defend a man against charges of murdering a wealthy widow.

The Wizard of Oz (1939)

Starring: Judy Garland, Frank Morgan, Ray Bolger. Director: Victor Fleming. Written by Noel Langley, Florence Ryerson, and Edgar Allan Woolf, adapted from the novel (*The Wonderful Wizard of Oz*) by L. Frank Baum; 101 minutes; Metro-Goldwyn-Mayer (MGM). While a tornado strikes, Dorothy, a teenager from Kansas, and her dog, Toto, are transported to a magical world.

Zulu (1964)

Starring: Stanley Baker, Jack Hawkins. Director: Cy Endfield. Written by John Prebble and Cy Endfield; 138 minutes; Diamond Films. In Africa during the late nineteenth century, a battalion of outnumbered English soldiers fights against the Zulus.

INDEX

ABOUT THE AUTHOR

David Mamet was born was born in Chicago in 1947. He studied at Goddard College in Vermont and at the Neighborhood Playhouse School of Theater in New York. He has taught at Goddard College, the Yale School of Drama, and New York University and lectures at the Atlantic Theater Company, of which he is a founding member. He is the author of the plays *The Cryptogram; Oleanna; Speed-the-Plow; Glengarry Glen Ross,* which was awarded the Pulitzer Prize; *American Buffalo;* and *Sexual Perversity in Chicago.* He has also written screenplays for such films as *House of Games* and the Oscar-nominated *The Verdict,* and *Wag the Dog,* as well as *The Spanish Prisoner, The Winslow Boy, Spartan,* and *Heist.*